Shakespeare: An Existential View

Shakespeare
An Existential View

David Horowitz

HILL AND WANG · New York

First published in Great Britain in 1965
by Tavistock Publications Limited
Copyright © 1965 by David Horowitz
All rights reserved

Library of Congress catalog card number 65-24720
First Edition October 1965

FOR ELISSA
who brings grace to my world

Manufactured in the United States of America
1 2 3 4 5 6 7 8 9 0

Contents

Contents

Acknowledgements

It is impossible to describe the profound way in which this book has been influenced by my teacher, Professor Andrew Chiappe of Columbia University. I have tried, by including a few fragments from his lectures, to indicate certain of the directions of this debt, but the current of his influence runs too deep to be so easily disclosed. Although the present work diverges from his teaching in both style and approach, his insights remain for me the way to an understanding of Shakespeare, and this book could not have been written without them.

I would also like to acknowledge the following debts: to Mr James Zito, of Columbia University, for his unstinting attention to my work as a student, and to Professor Jonas Barish, of the University of California, Berkeley, under whose guidance a first draft of the essay 'Imagining the Real' was written.

I have used the Arden Shakespeare for those plays for which it is available; elsewhere, I have used the edition of G. B. Harrison. All etymologies are taken from the O.E.D.

For their kind permission to quote passages from published works, thanks are due to: Faber and Faber Limited, in respect of *Shakespeare's Doctrine of Nature*, by John F. Danby; and John Murray (Publishers) Limited, in respect of *Religion and the Rise of Capitalism*, by R. H. Tawney.

Introduction

Every attempt to illuminate a work projects a light on to the object that is external to it and casts up shadows not its own. A successful illumination, therefore, can only be one that serves to reveal more than it obscures. In the end, the work itself is its own revelation.

To many, this book will seem an attempt to subject Shakespeare's brilliance to light from a particularly eccentric source. For existentialism is a modern outlook, Shakespeare a child of the Renaissance. By 'existential', however, I mean simply a view that proves itself in the reality of lived existence, not in the principles of metaphysical or theological discourse. Both existentialism and Renaissance humanism represent, in different periods and for different reasons, a return to the main Western tradition from the divergent stream of neo-Platonic (mainly Christian) thought. I have chosen to stress the 'existential' rather than the 'humanist' character of Shakespeare's outlook, because the word 'humanism' often carries with it overtones of an easy optimism that is absent from Shakespeare's work.

I am especially interested in preserving the complexity of Shakespeare's viewpoint, in this regard, because the underlying concern of the essays in this volume is to name the basis of Shakespearean optimism itself: to see what are for Shakespeare the springs of human grace and human creation, what the forces available for the repair of the tragic ruin and for the renewal of human life.

The second of the two essays addresses itself to the problem of the ethical foundations of human order, the relation between human values and human reality. It seeks, moreover, to show how the central tension in Shakespeare's tragic universe is rooted at least as deeply in the socio-economic tensions of the sixteenth century as in what is usually referred to as 'the Renaissance conflict', or the disintegration of the 'Elizabethan World Picture'.

The first of the two essays focuses on the relation between human vision and human realization, the relation between the mode in which men see reality and the manner in which they live it. The title is derived from an essay by Martin Buber, in which he defines the phrase 'imagining the real' to mean 'the capacity to hold before one's soul a reality arising at this moment but not able to be directly experienced', for example, the reality of another human consciousness. The meaning of the phrase in the context of the present essay is broader than in its particular use by Buber (though not than the usage suggested by his general writings), but its origin is the same: the fact that certain contours of the present and all the contours of the future are impenetrable to direct human experience.

The whole conception of this first essay has its origin in the perception that the way in which men imagine or conceive their worlds, and the way they bear themselves in them, are interdependent ways. To create is to make exist in reality what existed only in imagination before.

ONE

Imagining the Real

Man's heart designs designs in images
of the possible, which could be made
into the real.   *Martin Buber*

I

Imagination and Perception

I. ROMANTIC ENGAGEMENT AND SATIRIC DISENGAGEMENT

> What a piece of work is a man! how noble in reason!
> how infinite in faculty! in form and moving how express
> and admirable! in action how like an angel! in apprehen-
> sion how like a god! the beauty of the world! the paragon
> of animals! And yet, to me, what is this quintessence of
> dust?   (Hamlet)

The tensions between antithetic images of man, between 'divinity'
and 'dust', are not unique concerns of *Hamlet*, but form a focal
theme of the Shakespearean world experience. In high Shakespearean comedy, however, which is a proving ground for the
tragedies, this conflict of world views is modified by the lightness
of its context. Here, scepticism lacks that hysteria of despair which
characterizes it in its tragic setting, while its antithesis embodied in
comedy as chivalric romance is easily rendered ridiculous by being
stretched to shallow extremes.

In a post-romantic age the notion that, to appear absurd,
romanticism must first be made extreme, is not an obvious one.
To explore the conflict between scepticism and romance at the
heart of the Shakespearean perspective, therefore, it is necessary
first to examine the integrity of the romantic attitude.

The bearer of this attitude is an extravagant figure to begin
with, and because he has an exalted vision of reality and its possibilities, he is always in danger of over-reaching himself, of fleeing
barriers instead of vaulting them. But this peril is merely a peril

3

for him, and not a *predestination*. In its integrity, the romantic vision is more than fiction and answers to an experience that is authentic; there *are* rises in the human landscape that transcend the plain of mere physical action and decay. Love is such a transcendence and has its own language of being; it cannot be comprehended in the transactional terms of a prosaic world scheme.

For what is love but the binding of two strangers, who step forth to disclose themselves, withholding nothing and risking all? What binds lovers? What presents them to one another with such exclusiveness, brooking such commitment? And what moves them to exclude from their experience the whole world, except as it comes to them through the other? The hyperbole of romantic language and action answers to the hyperbole of love itself, and is the language adequate to this purpose.

Thus, death of the lovers, which is a fundamental figure in the romantic world image, signs the fact that love is absolute in a world of relatives: lovers must die to the world in order to be born to each other. The literature of cheap romance resolves this tension by rejecting the world; authentic romance lives the tension and, therefore, is tragic. But only romance as a language can express this paradox of an impossibility that is embodied, the paradox of love.

An exalted mode of living is not special to romantic experience in its restricted, amorous sense, and one speaks (even if in a modern patronizing fashion) of the romance of many other spheres of human action as well. Romance, in the Shakespearean context, has indeed such breadth; it is the defining character of every human way that is 'engaged', that has faith. From out of such faith (where 'faith' must be understood as a binding in relation, and not simply as belief*) meaning comes. For the one who is so bound, a certain structure of values is given or, rather, discloses itself as meaning, and this meaning not only supports, but is the mode of his being; the breaking of his faith breaks *him*.

* On the distinction between faith as 'trust' and faith as 'belief', see Martin Buber, *Two Types of Faith*, Routledge & Kegan Paul, London, 1951.

Religion, which in this sense is quintessential romance, is necessarily closed to attack from the outside, because its revelation and
its faith (the relation from which all meaning springs) stream forth
from a Being beyond the reality at hand. But, in romantic love,
revelation extends itself from a being whose outward form is
apprehensible to all. The foundations of belief in romantic love do
not involve factors beyond what seem to be accessible in the
actual lived reality that all men know (although the term 'know'
and the reality that is tied to it are themselves ultimately prob-
lematic). Romantic love, therefore, is at once open to criticism,
by a disengaged view, on the ground that it raises structures of
extravagant faith on foundations of mere earth, that meanings
which are absolute cannot be derived from phenomena which are
relative, which are situated within a temporal world order. Such
criticism in Shakespearean comedy can be witty and, at the same
time, profound.

Beatrice, an exponent of this scepticism in *Much Ado About
Nothing*, is single-minded in her pursuit of the non-divine founda-
tion of the marriage relation, the immanent basis of its bond of
absoluteness, and its essential absurdity in that light:

> LEONATO: Well, niece, I hope to see you one day fitted with
> a husband.
> BEATRICE: Not till God make men of some other metal than
> earth. Would it not grieve a woman to be overmaster'd
> with a piece of valiant dust? (II. 1)

Can one rest with such an extreme, if amusing, view of marriage
(and man), as is represented here, however, any more than one
can rest with only a single pole of Hamlet's dialectic? Indeed, the
very fact that there is a *dialectic*, a double human potential, reveals
something. It reveals that man is not a static but a dynamic being,
and hence, it cannot be said with finality that he is *either* noble *or*
bestial, that he *either* crowns the creation *or* merely settles on it as
an inconsequential dust. One can only say that man is the being
for whom such possibilities exist.

Moreover, man bears his consciousness of these possibilities, evaluates and makes decisions, in a kind of freedom. One can say, therefore, something about the relation between the realization of human possibilities and human consciousness of them, between the goals that man posits and the courses he pursues, between his created image of the world and his actual steps along its ways.

To speak about these questions with relevance to the Shakespearean context and the polarities that dominate it, one must speak in terms of 'romantic' and 'satiric' visions of the world. But this must be done now, from an ontological point of view.

For though romanticism can be regarded simply as an attempt to express in hyperbolic conception what is a hyperbolic experience, this is not its sole function. Like any ethical code, romanticism also answers to the task of lifting experience from the primitive level of its sources, of creating new forms of being. Thus, for example, the primitive source of love is sexuality, desire. But desire is a consuming force and by its nature cannot be sated: it seeks to consume, to destroy its object, that is, the very object which it desires. The romantic code understands this and sets out to restrain desire, or rather to redirect the energies of desire so that they come to a new focus. The quest of the lover centres now not simply on attaining, but on *serving*, the beloved, is directed not merely towards the other, but towards one's own being – to become worthy of love – and thus seeks its end not merely in the consummation of the relation, but in the relation itself, in the courtship, so that consummation, when it comes, is the consummation of something. And, indeed, love's consummation in civilized usage means climax – the flower of love – as well as the consuming of its fruit.

Thus, in the romantic vision, the reality of love as relation appears. Moreover, it *is* the vision of love as relation, as transcendent, that calls the reality to life. For he who sees in love only the sensual satisfaction of his lust, as a consequence of his perception (and the deed which springs from it) experiences only the sensual in his act.

6

Everywhere, value attends commitment. Where men do not address their condition in the fullness of its claim, there experience fails to cross the threshold of significance. For value can exist effectively only where there are men committed to it. It is the commitment of men to the possible, to what is loftier than their attainment, beyond what the present has achieved, that permits the realization of the potential whose seed is already there. 'In the realist, the miracle springs from faith, and not faith from the miracle' (Dostoevsky).

> Whether we take ... the Indo-Aryan *rita* ... the primeval order of that which is right and just, or Israel's *tsedek*, in which truth and justice combine, or the Greek *dike*, the inexorable course of world events, and the 'measure' determined by it – everywhere transcendent Being has a side facing toward man which represents a shall-be; *everywhere man, if he wants to exist as man, must strive after a super-human model. . . .'*

For all this, there is a Shakespearean language with its own special emphasis: where men recognize the bonds of claim and responsibility that bind them to other men, where commitment to values and relations stands above use and interest and the profit of self, where such commitment exists, the social and moral harmony of men is tuned, and the natural comes to fruition because its order has been preserved. But where the specialty of degree gives way to the specialty of interest, where the relations of men bow to the relations of commerce, where the bond of mercy is denied before the bond of trade, where the claims of humanity yield to the claims of self, there appetite, all that is left when the trappings have been stripped away, emerges, and this appetite, 'a universal wolf', makes everything its prey, until at last it eats up itself. All the refinements and values of civilization, all the significances and meanings of morality, rise out of the brute base to refine and ennoble it, and when all these have been stripped off, there is a bare, poor, forked animal, and no more. What lifts man beyond this? What stands to cover his nakedness? What to re-form his

* Buber, *At the Turning*, Farrar, Straus & Young, New York, 1952.

desire? Is it no more than mere illusion? To this question, the voice of the satiric disengagement answers with an emphatic *yes*.

That *yes* can be sounded with an emphasis that ranges from the frenzied bitterness of a Timon to the melancholic petulance of a Jaques. It has its paradigmatic expression in the answer of Diogenes the Cynic to the world conqueror from Macedon who had stopped in his way to ask the philosopher what he desired of him, Alexander. Diogenes answered that he wanted only that Alexander step aside and cease to block his sunlight.

Thus Diogenes' view is as relentless in its pursuit of the base clay on which all human enterprise is founded, as is Beatrice's; in the end, the world king Alexander is but a man, a piece of wayward marl; his offer to Diogenes can be nothing more than the offer of a man, nothing more than a man can offer: advancement among his fellow-men – the vanity that makes Alexander king and would make Diogenes his servant – or the material fulfilment of material desires, and in that case, what richer gift than sunlight?

Even as Diogenes' view of the human condition takes into its account only the physical stuff that men are made on, so Beatrice 'sees' only one truth: that man is a piece of valiant dust, not heroic, but a vainly strutting inconsequence. The already noted closeness of Beatrice's jibe to Hamlet's is in no way fortuitous, for the essential recognition of any philosophical scepticism as it poses for itself the question of man's significance, the point from which it always begins, is the fact of human mortality, of man's decay in time.

What separates Beatrice's statement from Hamlet's is not merely the focus of her point (which makes the issue light), but the main fact, that in his speech there is a dialectic of possibilities present. For he is caught between the sight of human potential, a potential that may come to realization in supreme moments and supreme individuals and, on the other side, the reality of man's condition, his corporeality and corruption, his domination by flesh and by time in the flesh, the inescapable decay that undermines and makes meaningless his project. The tragedy here is inexorable; its issue cannot be resolved, but only accepted, and in readiness, some way, for the particularity and uniqueness of each moment, redeemed.

It is this redemption and its real possibility that radical scepticism closes off. From a criticism that opposes itself to easy and therefore misleading solutions, a criticism that seeks to refine values and ideas, scepticism descends quickly into a position that negates the impulse to solution itself. This is the last illusion, an illusion that extends to itself no grace of possibility, and thus stifles in its own pride and dies. Such is the doom of Timon.

But just as the tragic treatment of romanticism differs from the comic, so, in comedy, scepticism can escape this end. But it can do this only by some transformation of its energy of negation. The study of such a transformation would provide an obvious opportunity to probe the sources of Shakespeare's optimism, the basis on which he rejects the dark vision and entertains the possibility of grace. Before approaching this point, however, it is first necessary to examine, concretely, Shakespeare's rejection of the shallow extremes of the two counter views.

Much Ado About Nothing is a play in which the sceptical and romantic views do confront one another, and in which there is also a positive transformation of the impulse towards negation. The contrast between world perspectives is experienced in this play in the lives of two pairs of lovers: Claudio and Hero, Benedick and Beatrice. Of these, Claudio and Hero seem to be the two who are involved, from the beginning, in a form of romantic experience. They seem to share in an exhilarating mode of being, an exalted reality, an existence informed with meaning and intense with values, all of which remain dark and unintelligible to the couple outside it.

Benedick's approach to love is oriented by the same intuition as Beatrice's, namely, that the object of love's religion is a being that has no presence of the divine in it:

BENEDICK: I will not be sworn but love may transform me to an oyster, but I'll take my oath on it, till he have made an oyster of me, he shall never make me such a fool: one

> woman is fair, yet I am well: another virtuous, yet I am
> well: but till all graces be in one woman, one woman shall
> not come in my grace: . . .   (II. 3)

To be worthy of worship a woman ought to embody all graces,
for otherwise the worshipper degrades his own being, and becomes an oyster. For by worshipping a mortal he shifts the divine
down to the human, thus displacing the whole cosmic scale and
relegating himself to the very bottom of the great chain of being.
Conversely, such a degradation of one's being can only attend the
attrition of one's reason; only a man who has become an oyster,
that is mere sense without the slightest glint of reason, could permit himself to be made such a fool.

The faculty of reason fends off the indignity of love, and it does
so by annihilating the very notion of a 'love' which is more than
'lust'. For reason, unaided, cannot 'see' any potential in what is
sensual to be more than sensual, or in man, to be more than man.
Reason and its instrument logic, however, must themselves be
scrutinized with care. As Hero observes of Beatrice in the play:

> HERO: . . . I never yet saw man,
>   How wise, how noble, young, how rarely featured,
>   But she would spell him backward: if fair-faced
>   She would swear the gentleman should be her sister:
>   If black, why, Nature, drawing of an antic,
>   Made a foul blot: if tall, a lance ill-headed:
>   If low, an agate very vilely cut: . . .
>   So turns she every man the wrong side out,
>   And never gives to truth and virtue that
>   Which simpleness and merit purchaseth.
>
> (III. 1)

If it is set to do so, rational analysis, i.e. reason, may annihilate any
attitude towards experience, merely by shifting its assumptions.
For analytic reason needs assumptions in order to proceed, and its
whole subsequent direction depends on those assumptions. Reason,
of necessity therefore, falls into illusion when it seeks to judge what
is outside the limits of its own experience (e.g. love) and therefore

outside the sphere where its axioms have their validity, where its constructs make sense. On the other hand, reason cannot by itself extend its own limits, because in order to do this it would have to open itself to the experience of that which is beyond them; it would have to relinquish its own position, that is, relinquish itself. It is Benedick, ironically, who touches this paradox of being unable to be both 'inside' and 'outside' an experience (a necessary capability for any complete analysis of human events):

> BENEDICK: Well, every one can master a grief, but he that has it. (III. 2)

When, in the course of the play, reason capitulates before experience, it does so because it is a reason of appearances, of what has already been experienced, but not of what is yet to be experienced. Its defect is the defect of being on the 'outside', for analytic reason can view events only at a distance, and hence, while it may exert control over them, cannot participate in their making.

The satiric and essentially analytic stance of Benedick and Beatrice, which does not yet know relation, is not capable of the perception that it is from the relation itself that value springs, a value not wholly present in the object or *devotio* alone, but one arising with the relation. When Benedick and Beatrice discover this, they discover, too, that the uniqueness of the relation between them is as closed to others as others' relations were closed to them. Claudio's shallow romanticism shares, in fact, in the same error (missing the power of relation), but it does so from an opposite pole – not because it fixes too absolutely on the other, but because it does not 'see' the other at all; it knows only itself and its 'feeling':

> DON PEDRO: . . . Dost thou affect her, Claudio?
> CLAUDIO: O my Lord,
>   When you went onward on this ended action,
>   I looked upon her with a soldier's eye,
>   That lik'd but had a rougher task in hand
>   Than to drive liking to the name of love:
>   But now I am return'd and that war-thoughts
>   Have left their places vacant, in their rooms

Come thronging soft and delicate desires,
All prompting me how fair young Hero is,
Saying I lik'd her ere I went to wars. (I. 1)

Claudio is in love with love, as he had been in love with war prior
to that ('I have known him when he would have walk'd ten mile
afoot to see a good armour, and now will he lie ten nights awake
carving the fashion of a new doublet' – Benedick). Because his
own feeling is primary for him Claudio's central concern is
whether Hero is worthy of his love, whereas (from a chivalric
point of view) it ought to be whether his love is worthy of her:

CLAUDIO: Benedick, didst thou note the daughter of Signior
Leonato?
BENEDICK: I noted her not; but I look'd on her . . .
CLAUDIO: Thou think'st I am in sport: I pray thee tell me
truly how thou lik'st her.
BENEDICK: Would you buy her, that you inquire after her?

Benedick's jibe is penetrating and apt. The true man of faith
(where 'faith' is to be understood not as 'a feeling in the soul of
man, but rather an entrance into the whole of reality, without
reduction and curtailment'*) is committed in spite of the world's
judgement, not in deference to it. As Beatrice elsewhere says, ''Tis
the world's fashion to avoid cost.' And Borachio: 'Seest thou not
what a deformed thief this fashion is.' 'Fashion' is a term relating
to the world of opinions and appearances, 'faith', to a reality
deeper than that which is open generally and to all men. The
martyr dies for his faith in what is unseen by the many, the lover
lives for it. Benedick understands this, in his witty way, even as
Claudio does not:

CLAUDIO: That I love [Hero], I feel.
DON PEDRO: That she is worthy, I know.
BENEDICK: That I neither feel how she should be loved, nor
know how she should be worthy, *is the opinion that fire
cannot melt out of me: I will die in it at the stake.*

* Buber, *Eclipse of God*, New York, Harper & Bros, 1952.

The real failure of a shallow romanticism is that its romance is not a romance of life, but of romance itself, its faith not a binding in reality, but a flight from it. Shallow romanticism abstracts from life, takes form for content, makes a substance of mere shows, and exists – in so far as it exists at all – only as a fiction, as a dream of passion, not a lived response to the concreteness of real beings and things.

A pair of parallel scenes in *Much Ado* discloses the failure of shallow romanticism to tie itself to the lived concrete:

> DON PEDRO: I do but stay till your marriage be consummate, and then go I toward Arragon.
>
> CLAUDIO: I'll bring you thither, my Lord, if you'll vouchsafe me.
>
> DON PEDRO: Nay, that would be as great a soil in the new gloss of your marriage as to show a child his new coat and forbid him to wear it. . . .   (III. 2)

Claudio's offer to desert his bride on their marriage morning reveals symbolically, as well as in fact, the lack of substance in what has been his love-suit, the essential emptiness, the fantasy nature of his movement towards his Hero (and Don Pedro's imagery of child and cloak does not fail to mark this).

This exchange might not be so noteworthy were it not matched with another involving the second figure of this romantic pair. As she puts on her wedding dress, Hero has the following conversation with her servant Margaret:

> HERO: God give me joy to wear it! for my heart is exceeding heavy.
>
> MARGARET: 'Twill be heavier soon by the weight of a man.
>
> HERO: Fie upon thee! art not ashamed?
>
> MARGARET: Of what lady? of speaking honourably? is not marriage honourable in a beggar? is not your lord honourable without marriage? I think you would have me say, saving your reverence, a husband: and bad thinking do not wrest true speaking, I'll offend nobody: is there any harm in the heavier for a husband?   (III. 4)

Hero has not understood what is involved in marriage; she has not wanted to face the fact that it means being heavier by the weight of a man. Hero's conception of marriage, abhorring as it does real contact, would in theory welcome Claudio's proposed desertion; in fact, it is its counterpart. Moreover, this very distance in reality between them, a distance which their manner of romance encourages, combines with their religicized but only apparent closeness to make possible the catastrophe that later engulfs them; for were their attitudes towards one another founded on a more concrete intimacy, they would not be such easy prey for the illusions that are conjured up to separate them, and were they less prone to theologizing experience, Hero's supposed misconduct could not attain the stature of damnation-headed heresy that it does. Indeed, the near 'tragedy' that overtakes Hero and Claudio is set on a stage of extravagant self-deception, which contrasts radically with the daylight realism of Beatrice and Benedick; it is this realism, moreover, which knits together the tough fabric of the subsequent romance of this sceptical pair. For the strength of their relation stems precisely from its consciousness. In love, which as they live it is authentic romance, they are faithful not only to each other and to the meaning of their love, but to themselves:

> Benedick and Beatrice rail at each other, which is proper for civilized people in love, because love implies the greatest of indignities to be suffered: to give oneself. (Chiappe)

But this is to anticipate. Before examining the transformation of the sceptical disengagement of Beatrice and Benedick, it is necessary to see its limits. To do this, it is helpful to consider the parallel figure of a fellow-sceptic, Jaques, in *As You Like It*.

The extreme of the satirical view (and hence its fulfilment) is expressed in Jaques's picture of man's pageant through life as a procession from the stage of puking, whining, and sighing, to making ballads on ladies' eyebrows, to the quest for a mere bubble – reputation – through the satisfaction of a round belly, 'full of wise saws and modern instances' playing at justice, to the bespectacled wispish echo, who 'pipes and whistles in his sound', shuffles through 'a world too wide for his shrunk shank' decked in 'youthful hose well-sav'd', until he reaches his final condition: 'mere oblivion, sans teeth, sans eyes, sans taste, sans everything'. Life as a project towards nothing and a nothing project, an empty show – life as the progress of mere sensuality which dresses itself in a pageant of vacuous fraudulent gestures and vain quests and, as a result, attains its own absurdity as its significance – this is the ultimate negative view, the final extension of the satiric probe. (It is no mere coincidence, of course, that Jaques gets his name from a 'jakes', i.e. a privy. For this superbly symbolizes his view and his function, and his creator's conception of both.)

The perilous closeness of Benedick's unrelenting critique of fond illusions to Jaques's negation of the possibility of any authentic or significant activity at all, is evidenced in their parallel attitudes towards music. Music is a touchstone in considering rationalist and 'irrationalist' views, for music is a something in experience to which an intuition or faculty different from 'cool reason' responds. It is an edifice that the spirit itself raises over merely physical experience to transform it:

Enter Balthazar with music. . . .
BENEDICK: Now, divine air, now is his soul ravish'd! Is it not strange that sheep's guts should hale souls out of men's bodies?

For Benedick, the name of the music describes its reality. It is an air, that is, nothing.

This is the characteristic direction of the satiric view of experience: to dwell on the physical and to reduce everything to it (to see reality here only in the fact that sheep guts are being plucked), to deny the capacity of the physical to rise beyond itself except as mere illusion. Benedick refuses to note notes that are mere nothings. The idea of harmony, a structuring of sounds that elicits from them a new significance, is apparently as closed to him as is the suggestion that there may be other harmonies, a structuring of human relations, or of relations within the self, which in these spheres, too, transforms realities and can make, of something like mere animal guts, a song.

The rejection of music involves more than symbolic significances; it is a rejection of joy and celebration, the very triumphs that life does – above and despite all – afford. For dancing and music are ways to celebrate life's feasts, wherever such feasts spring momentarily into being, before the inevitable shifting of time causes them to dissolve and pass away. Jaques leaves a marriage celebration which Duke Senior has begun, with these words:

> DUKE: Play, music! and you, brides and bridegrooms all,
>   With measure heap'd in joy, to the measures fall . . .
> JAQUES: . . . so to your pleasures,
>   I am for other than for dancing measures.   (v. 4)

What is being rejected here is something within experience that rises above it, something that transforms it and makes it a subject for praise. Celebration itself is built over what is merely present. Man brings celebration to being; he alone of creatures is capable of celebration, and the feast, which is momentarily possible for him, is possible only for as long as he sustains it.

'I can suck melancholy out of a song as a weasel sucks eggs', Jaques says earlier. The egg in his phrase signs the significance behind these perceptions. For in the egg – which shows forth only eggness, mere food to weasels and to him – is a bird; and the mystery of the bird's lodging in the egg and the miracle of his becoming from it, is a metaphor for the mystery of joy and the wonder of its birth from man's cold and melancholic condition.

II. NOTING APPEARANCES AND REALITIES

> May I be so converted and see with these eyes?
>   (Benedick)

The sceptical realism of the satiric disengagement flails at the extravagance of the romantic vision, and with relentless energies seeks to winnow the brute fact from experience. But because it sifts out all that does not meet its condition of real physical presence, it never steps into confrontation with the whole of what is accessible and reachable in the world, or with what may emerge as a content within it.

The career of Don Quixote (albeit an 'obsessed' romantic) illustrates how a critical realism that will not see what is unseen, misses the potential in reality to become something else, and in this way misses reality itself. For if, with those who are opposed to Don Quixote, you see only what man is (that is, what he has been) then you do not fully see man, because you do not see what he might be. That is why the 'madness' of Don Quixote is perception, and his quest heroic, while the 'sanity' of those who surround him is in an important sense blind to realities, to the possibility of noble action.

Don Quixote's view is faithful to a nobility that might be, to a nobility that by his own action he makes exist, that he (to use a Sartrean construction) *exists*. Under the pressure of his vision, 'nobility' is no longer potential: it *is*. By contrast, the view that mocks Don Quixote, being faithful only to the limited reality of what generally appears, exerts no pressure on 'reality', but rests in this limit as its end.

The fault is not Don Quixote's if no one follows him. His view of the world is extravagant, but is not in its essence impossible. He is committed to what is noble in life, to every valued principle of social man, to truth, to honour, to justice, to the protection of the helpless against the strong, to the sense of the intense, rich experience of living – all of which is seized in the symbol of the golden age that is to come again.

It is precisely this perception of the world's heroic potential, moreover, that gives Don Quixote the capacity to live heroically. Vision, faith in his vision, and the will to answer it, to act on it, give him all his power. And, indeed, in all literature there is no figure more heroic than he, precisely because he is heroic with only this power, heroic, as it is given to every man to be – alone, in his integrity and grace.

Thus it is fitting that the great moment in Don Quixote's life, the climax of his career, is the moment of his defeat by the

Knight of the White Moon. Committed, as he is, to the chivalric code, a code binding him to his word, he is required to submit to the conditions that his conqueror sets for him. And to every condition that the Knight of the White Moon sets (even to giving up his knightly calling) he submits, but one.

The Knight of the White Moon* bids him admit that Dulcinea del Toboso is not the most beautiful lady in the world, that she is, indeed, not fairer than any woman. Here, at the door to this betrayal, Don Quixote sets the limits of his submission and defeat. Though in refusing this point he yields up his life (a sacrifice that is not taken), he remains firm. His commitment to his lady, to the truth of his vision of her, a truth that was the source of his strength throughout his career and the inspiration for his service, stands above all other values for him. He cannot preserve his life and yield up this vision, for to yield up the vision is to die out of the world in which he has lived (and this is of course the meaning of his subsequent 'death' by 'sanity'). To the Knight of the White Moon's command that he declare Dulcinea ugly, his truth and its beauty dead, the answer of the shamed and beaten knight, an absurd, bedraggled, ridiculous old man, is *no*.

Who is Dulcinea? By other eyes she is seen as a coarse, sweaty peasant girl, cruel to Don Quixote in their only confrontation, and oblivious to his service. What then stands between them, and what is asserted in his heroic gesture? It is the perception of the potential in every woman to be Dulcinea del Toboso to one man, to be most beautiful to him, and in her loveliness, to ennoble him, moving him to high service and to heroic actions. Dulcinea *is* his inspiration, hers is the spirit that moves in him; she is the symbol of his vision of the world, of a world, moreover, which has momentarily become this vision – the scene of authentic 'golden' nobility – by virtue of his golden deeds.

---

* The moon, of course, represents inconstancy.

Benedick, didst thou note the daughter of Signior Leonato?
I noted her not; but I looked on her.

Note notes, forsooth, and nothing.

(*Much Ado About Nothing*)

The term for perception in *Much Ado* is 'noting'. To 'note' is to take note of, to note specially, to set down in the memory, to pay serious attention to; a 'noting' is a special kind of perception therefore. Such a perception may yield more than is seen by merely looking and, therefore, from the point of view of the satiric disengagement and its relentless realism, less. The term itself suggests this possibility, because the Elizabethans sounded the word 'noting' the same way as 'nothing' (i.e. both words were *noting*).

Early in the action of *Much Ado*, Don Pedro meets Benedick moments after Claudio has left him. Claudio has been complaining of his supposed betrayal by the prince (a betrayal suggested by experience which has been falsely noted to him). Benedick engages the prince in a discussion of this betrayal and Claudio's reaction to it (in order presumably to clear things up), but the prince mis-notes his words and misses his meaning, and the misunderstanding between them goes unpatched for the time being:

BENEDICK: I told him [Claudio], and I think I told him true, that your Grace had got the good will of this young lady.

(II. 1)

The prince notes a meaning in these words that Benedick does not intend, namely, that his graciousness had got the goodwill of the young lady for Claudio (for Don Pedro had previously indicated that he would intervene on Claudio's behalf). Benedick, of course, means quite the opposite. He means that his Grace, i.e. Don Pedro, had won the favour of Hero for himself. Thus, a nothing meaning, a meaning that was not intended, becomes the whole meaning, and obscures the sense of the speech.

It is this kind of error, in fact, that dominates the major actions of the play, especially those leading up to the near tragedy of

Claudio and Hero; for the way to this misfortune is paved entirely by 'events' which are misnoted notings (nothings). Hence the title of the play with its *double entendre*: Much Ado About Not(h)ing.

The 'tragedy' of the play is triggered when Claudio and Don Pedro note an experience, namely, the presence of two figures (Borachio and Margaret) in Hero's chamber, that is not an experience at all, because it is something other than what they take it to be. They take the scene to be evidence that Hero has betrayed Claudio. They do this, because Don John, who has created the scene, notes it to them in a special way. He has created not only the scene (for he has instructed Borachio in what to do) but its significance as well, which he does by naming or noting the characters to the audience (Claudio and Don Pedro): this shadow is Hero. But this shadow is not Hero. Noted differently, the experience is a mere nothing.

Not surprisingly for a play whose central action turns on such an incident, *Much Ado* is persistent in its pursuit of the question of appearances. In the beginning, Claudio notes the appearance of more sweetness and modesty in Hero than does Benedick: 'Can the world buy such a jewel?' he says; but only a short time later he is ready to believe that she has been won by Don Pedro and so bids every eye 'negotiate for itself', for 'beauty is a witch'. Later, after he imagines he has 'seen' himself betrayed again, he can note in her blushes only 'guiltiness, not modesty':

> CLAUDIO: You seem to me as Dian in her orb,
> As chaste as is the bud ere it be blown:
> But you are more intemperate in your blood
> Than Venus, or those pamp'red animals
> That rage in savage sensuality.   (IV. I)

He no longer notes what she appears (which now seems to have no significance for him) but what she 'is':

> O Hero, what a Hero hadst thou been,
> If half thy outward graces had been placed
> About thy thoughts and counsels of thy heart!

But fare thee well, most foul, most fair! farewell.
Thou pure impiety, thou impious purity.

If Claudio, so certain of the truth of appearances earlier and, indeed, resting his case on a shadowy set of appearances even here when he denounces Hero at the marriage altar, is sure that the outward show does not sign anything that is inward, there are others present in the scene who take the opposite view. Benedick, for one, noting all the bitterness and cruelty, the seeming deception of Hero, the vindictiveness of her beloved, remarks with cutting irony (at the same time probing the fact that these have been lovers of style): 'This looks not like a nuptial.'

Another and more serious support of the view that sees more than mere superficiality in the surface of things is also voiced in these painful proceedings:

FRIAR: Hear me a little:
    For I have only been silent so long,
    And given way to this course of fortune,
    By noting of the lady: I have mark'd
    A thousand blushing apparitions
    To start into her face, a thousand innocent shames
    In angel whiteness beat away those blushes,
    And in her eye there hath appear'd a fire
    To burn the errors that these princes hold
    Against her maiden truth.

For the Friar, the truth is written on Hero's face. Earlier, in another context, Benedick has declared: 'knavery cannot sure hide itself in such reverence' (II. 3), and despite the irony here because of the situation, there is a distinct echo of Ursula's neo-Platonic formula: 'Can virtue hide itself? Go to, mum, you are he: graces will appear and there's an end.' The play, in other words, is as relentlessly 'for' the view that appearances are the whole of reality (or at least accurately reflect reality) as it is 'for' the contrary position, that appearances are deceptions, at best, not to be trusted. The question is a complex one, its issues intricate and involved.

One measure of this complexity is the way in which the play's ironies are pushed to greater and greater extremes as the play proceeds. The mechanism of the climactic action is a set of false appearances taken for real ones. Evil, in the person of Don John, makes no direct physical assault upon its victims; it merely manipulates the surface of things, making falsehoods appear true (which, of course, is the primal deed of Satan in the Garden). Real harm, then, is not done by the deceiver, but by the deceived. Similarly, Claudio's good intentions are transformed into an evil deed, not by an active will, but by a transformed sight. It is an altered appearance of reality that transforms his love to hate, his innocence to guilt.

Ironically, however, at the crucial point he fails to save himself and his Hero from their fate, by failing to repeat his procedure and take appearances (now Hero's blushes of innocence as he denounces her) for reflected realities. Thus, Claudio continually misreads the significance of surfaces (which he notes, however, as accurately as circumstances seem to permit) and hence misconceives the realities hidden underneath.

By contrast, the guardians of reality (and hence, innocence) in this play, namely, Dogberry and the Watch, note nothing accurately on the surface of things, but everything underneath. Dogberry is afflicted with a malaprop sense of language that effectively garbles the appearance (and hence the reality) not only of what he says, but of what he hears. It is, in fact, a provident co-ordination of these disabilities that enables Dogberry and the Watch to disentangle appearances and present the main figures of the drama with reality revealed.

The Watch does not 'see' the evil that is done (indeed, there is nothing evil to 'see') but overhears it. Borachio, explaining to Conrade how he and Margaret had appeared in the window of Hero's chamber and how Don John had deliberately misinterpreted the scene to his brother (Don Pedro) and Claudio, is overheard by the Watch saying:

> . . . chiefly by my villainy, which did confirm any slander that Don John had made, away went Claudio enrag'd . . . (III. 3)

The Watch mishears what Borachio has said (he thinks that Borachio has said that Don John is a villain) and misinterprets its significance; thus, Borachio is arrested not for the deed which he has confessed, but for slandering Don John, the prince's brother. The Watch has apprehended the right man, for the wrong reason.

This error is corrected, however, when the Watch reports to Dogberry what he has heard. For Dogberry outdoes his subordinate (as is only proper) in seeming incompetence by repeating his error of misnoting what he hears:

> 1 WATCH: This man said, sir, that Don John, the prince's brother, was a villain.
> DOGBERRY: Write down Prince John a villain. . . . (IV. 2)

Thus, by a process of double negation, the truth is brought to the surface. In other words, a consistently wrong sense of appearances may produce as true a picture of reality as a consistently right one. Indeed, in a world where appearances are deliberately manipulated to imply false realities, only a false sense of (false) appearances can register the truth of events.

In an exquisite and witty moment later on, the tangles of the plot, the confused surfaces and depths, confront each other in an essential way:

> DOGBERRY: Marry, sir, they have committed false report, moreover they have spoken untruths, secondarily they are slanders, sixth and lastly they have belied a Lady, thirdly they have verified unjust things, and to conclude, they are lying knaves.
> DON PEDRO: First I ask thee what they have done: thirdly I ask thee what's their offence; sixth and lastly why they are committed; and, to conclude, what you lay to their charge.
> CLAUDIO: Rightly reasoned, and in his own division, and by my troth there's one meaning well suited. (V. 1)

Dogberry is speaking about Conrade and Borachio, but what he says is strictly applicable (with the possible exception of the concluding point) to Don Pedro and Claudio. Thus, when Claudio says 'there's one meaning well suited', his statement has the double sense of one meaning 'put into many dresses' (Dr Johnson) and more importantly, of one meaning appropriate to himself and Don Pedro, as well as to Conrade and Borachio. Thus a diversity of appearances (Dogberry's words) may have one meaning, or significance, while the surface significance of a single meaning (Claudio's statement) may be double.

From this brief rehearsal of themes it is evident that the play raises many more questions than it expects (or can be expected) to answer. But these questions are not primarily raised to be answered. Nor are they simply rhetorical. They serve, rather, an attempt to evoke the special multiple quality of human experience, when probed by an ontological point of view. The issues raised by this attempt cannot be simply summed; but they are implicated (and stunningly so) in a question asked by Dogberry, as he opens the interrogation scene which unravels the entangled matter of the key sequence of misappearances in the play. The question points not only to the moment at hand, but to the larger movement of the play itself:

Is our whole dissembly appear'd? (IV. 2)

From out of what may be called the play's dissemblage, there emerges more than simple confusion, however. For the play's actions demonstrate not only that the relation between appearance and reality is a sometimes tenuous and always complex one, but also that, because of this uncertainty at the centre of experience, reality is in a large sense what men make it.

2

Imagination and Realization

I. MULTIPLE PERSPECTIVE

The whole sequence of misnoted events, and the resulting complex of misdirected responses, in *Much Ado* thus points to the conclusion that phenomenal reality, the reality appearing to men, is the reality that they apprehend – reality, for them, differs with their differing stances towards their condition. For 'reality' is no thing, but a *world* – or better still, *worlds* – not single and opaque, but multiple and opalescent.

In *Much Ado*, this protean world character expresses itself as a multiplicity of appearances and responses to appearances; in a sister play, *Twelfth Night, Or, What You Will*, as multiple pleasures and wills to pleasure. Just as a large view enriches experience, so a narrow view is a limiting one, confining life possibilities:

> Dost thou think because thou art virtuous there will be no
> more cakes and ale?   (Sir Toby)

Therefore, the dialectic of views represented by the two pairs of lovers in *Much Ado* is not resolved by rejecting one for the other, by discarding the romantic perspective for its antithesis. Despite both the failure of Claudio and Hero to navigate a true course, and the corresponding success of the critical pair Benedick and Beatrice, the survival of romance as a viable world-image in the play is assured. It is assured not only by the shallowness of the romantic couple which limits the implications of their actions, but by the final romantic 'conversion' of Benedick and Beatrice.

When the deluded Claudio denies Hero at the altar, he is in a sense denying her for the second time. Earlier, when he is falsely led to believe that Don Pedro has usurped his place and wooed Hero for himself, Claudio shows a readiness to be rid of his Hero that calls into question the very existence of a bond of faith between them:

BENEDICK: . . . the Prince hath got your Hero.
CLAUDIO: I wish him joy of her.
BENEDICK: Why, that's spoken like an honest drovier. So they sell bullocks. . . . (II. 1)

To be sure, Claudio speaks out of bitterness. But Benedick's daylight perception is finely tuned to the contours of reality and this is not the first time that he has likened Claudio's attachment to Hero to a commodity relation. (It is worth remembering, in this regard, that the first inquiry Claudio makes about Hero is whether she is Leonato's heir.)

Now, the central fact about a commodity relation is that it is one-sided, the relation of a person to a thing, the one an active possessor, the other a passive possession. The value of the possession, moreover, is inconstant, as is its relation to the person who buys it; a change in its market value may induce him to sell or perhaps even discard it.

Love is the antithesis of this kind of relation. Love is two-sided and therefore, in love, value is not external to, but springs from, the relation. It is not that the lovers possess no merit, no value in themselves, but this value is an active force in each of them that seizes and inspires and draws them together towards possibilities they did not have before. Their relation, therefore, does not remain external to their beings, but they give and hazard all they have. For love involves their very destinies in its 'contract', which does not fluctuate with fortune, but is 'a world-without-end bargain'.

Claudio's denunciation of Hero at the altar reflects the 'commercial' one-sided nature of his bond. She has become worthless in his eyes and he has resolved to kill her as a thing of value in all men's eyes, even as she has been killed in his own. Her 'death' affects nothing but herself. Claudio loses a jewel, whose value he has been deceived about, but that is all. His world remains intact. In other words, love for him has been no compass, no direction; he has remained outside the sphere of genuine romantic existence, and merely appropriated its rhetoric. Religious symbols provide frills for his experience, but no defining metaphor for his love: to come to the altar for Claudio is simply a ceremonious coming to market.

Claudio's attitude contrasts sharply with that of the true romantic, whose love is a religion and the shattering of whose faith is indeed a shattering of faith, a failure not of mere belief but of the human condition itself, the untuning of cosmic harmonies and the inverting of universal orders. When a romantic like Othello imagines himself betrayed, he speaks in accents of despair which are unmistakable:

> OTHELLO: But I do love thee; and when I love thee not
> Chaos is come again—   (III. 3)

'Chaos' is both chaos of his being and the disintegration of his world, a return to primal emptiness. For his love is both the pretext and source of his power, the orientation of his life deed, performed in service of his love.

Othello's love is both origin and destination; he is defined by its compass; its loss deprives him of his role, his 'occupation', his very being. In a more than metaphorical sense, his love is the wellspring of his life:

> OTHELLO: But there where I have garnered up my heart,
> Where I must either live or bear no life,
> The fountain from which my current runs,
> Or else dries up – to be discarded thence!   (IV. 2)

The venture of love is absolute ('My life upon her faith'). In its binding lovers find the measure of all values; it *bestows* value, and grace:

> . . . were I crown'd the most imperial monarch
> Thereof most worthy, were I the fairest youth

That ever made eye swerve, had force and knowledge
More than was ever man's, I would not prize them
Without her love; for her, employ them all;
Commend them and condemn them to her service,
Or to their own perdition.

(Florizel, The Winter's Tale, IV. 4)

To find corruption here, is to find everything corrupt; for every-thing has been measured against this divinity and found wanting. If such prove false, then none can be true. The 'fall' inverts all values and significances: divine Desdemona becomes 'fair *devil*', the Heaven of Othello's marriage chamber becomes darkest Hell, the deceiver Iago* supplants the honest Desdemona as Othello's betrothed ('I am your own forever') and the issue of his marriage is not life, but death.

All this is experience which Claudio remains outside of, throughout his own ordeal. His essential order of reality is not touched by the 'exposure' of his beloved. Though he vows to suspect all beauty henceforth, he experiences no elemental crisis, no compulsion to transfer or preserve his faith. The source of his calm lies in the fact that his original bond with Hero was a surface bond, not a faith; his order of reality *originally* remained unaffected (he merely transferred an affection from war to love) and for that reason, through the crisis, can be maintained intact. What destroys Othello, is that he loves Desdemona even after she has 'betrayed' him ('Be thus when thou art dead, and I will kill thee and love thee after'). What differentiates Claudio absolutely from Othello is that he has no *need*, even, of preservation; for though he may have fancied Hero, he has never really loved her.

Indeed, Claudio's whole apprehension of Hero has, from its inception, stopped at the surface:

> CLAUDIO: In mine *eye* she is the sweetest lady that ever I looked on. (I. I)

When he first feels that she has betrayed him (with Don Pedro) the lesson he gleans is 'Let every *eye* negotiate for itself',

* Iago – James – Jacob – the supplanter (Chiappe).

and the central deception practised upon him is thus aptly instrumented:

> BORACHIO: . . . I have deceived even your very eyes. . . .
> (V. 1)

In the fact that Claudio's sense of Hero is never more than superficial, his suit is revealed to be not love's but fancy's:

> Tell me where is Fancy bred,
> In the heart or in the head?
> How begot, how nourished? . . .
> It is engender'd in the eyes,
> With gazing fed, and Fancy dies
> In the cradle where it lies:
> Let us all ring Fancy's knell.
> I'll begin it. Ding, dong, bell.
> (Song in The Merchant of Venice, III. 2)

Benedick and Beatrice, who have been caustically critical of love in general and each other in particular, are brought together by the second major elaborate deception of the play. Separately, they are made to overhear reports concerning the transformation of each other's feelings. Benedick's first reaction to the intelligence that Beatrice loves him is: 'This can be no trick.' Since he thinks that he is overhearing a conversation which was not meant for his ears (he is concealed), the very suspicion that it might be a trick is stronger than the denial itself and thus, as an intuition, is particularly well tuned. The irony of the situation is, of course, double. For the deception of Benedick is only a surface deception. Benedick and Beatrice really are in love, and Benedick's readiness to accept the intelligence of the 'deception' reveals the extent to which his perspective comprehends the possibility of this love. He is not surprised to find that his severest critic is his truest admirer. For the one is a function of the other, and Benedick and Beatrice have all along, and in the deepest sense, been concerned with each other. Benedick, in the end, is right: this can be no trick.

Benedick's intuition into the 'truth' of his experience rests not only on deep self-knowledge, but on a corresponding awareness of the character whom he must rely on to perceive and interpret events for him. It is, in fact, Hero's father Leonato who confirms the (false) report of the evidence of Beatrice's love for Benedick. Noting from whose lips the intelligence comes, Benedick concludes: 'Sure, knavery cannot hide itself in such reverence.' And he is right. This is not knavery, but a well-meaning trick based on an accurate perception about himself and Beatrice, and motivated by a benevolent intention towards them.

By contrast, Claudio depends for his 'intelligence' on the bastard Don John, who is unscrupulous and has reason to wish to do harm to Claudio and the Prince. Indeed, when the Friar suggests that the three who claim to have 'seen' Hero's perfidy have been deceived in some way, Benedick quickly locates the source of the deception. He notes that two of them (Claudio and Don Pedro):

> . . . have the very bent of honour
> And if their wisdoms be misled in [regard to Hero]
> The practice of it lies in John the bastard,
> Whose spirits toil in the frame of villainies.   (IV. 1)

Thus, the very attention to concrete details which characterizes the satiric vision, enables Benedick to sort out appearance from reality; and, conversely, it is Claudio's romantic penchant for projecting his vision away from the concrete, for adorning the mundane with fantastic suits, that prevents him from seeing truly.

Notwithstanding that they have begun their relation within the context of a complex set of appearances (they have been mutual antagonists – they have merely heard reports of each other's affection), Benedick and Beatrice come quickly to the firm ground of real engagement, and to the mutual confrontation which attends that arrival.

Their declarations of love follow on the disgrace of Hero and are precipitated by Beatrice's distress over this event, which

Benedick seeks to salve. Benedick's first avowal is couched in accents which, while certainly romantic, remain true to his original mode:

> BENEDICK: I do love nothing in the world so well as you.
> Is that not strange? (IV. I)

This formulation in the negative provides a kind of cover for his nakedness, giving an impression of reasonableness that the more orthodox – 'I love you more than anything' – would not have. But Beatrice remains non-committal.

> BENEDICK: By my sword, Beatrice, thou lovest me.
> BEATRICE: Do not swear and eat it.

He cannot compel her into love. It is her grace to give him, and he knows it. He can swear for her, but confirm it only for himself:

> BENEDICK: I will swear by it that you love me, and I will make him eat it that says I love not you.
> BEATRICE: Will you eat your word?
> BENEDICK: With no sauce that can be devised to it. I protest I love thee.

This naked avowal satisfies Beatrice and she responds, wittily at first; then openly:

> BEATRICE: I love you with so much of my heart that none is left to protest.

Her gift is grace. His answer acknowledges it and seals, moreover, the basic loss of his cherished singleness. He has given his heart away:

> BENEDICK: Come, bid me do anything for thee.

This is the true romantic gesture, the confirmation in deed of the transcendent value of the relation. Love here manifests itself as a real force in the world, as the absolute source of direction, as ultimate significance. She takes him at his word:

> BEATRICE: Kill Claudio.

Love is immediately the basis for decision over life itself. Beatrice's love for Hero determines her decision; Benedick's love for Beatrice must determine his. Her command, accordingly, is absolute, as absolute as the bond which they have sealed, as absolute as its horizon, which is death.

BENEDICK: Ha! Not for the wide world.
BEATRICE: You kill me to deny it. Farewell.

The bond that is between them is a word only, and can never be more than a word. Benedick has seemed to give content to this word – 'Come, bid me do anything for thee' – but now he withdraws what he has given, *breaks* his word and, in Beatrice's eyes, its substance. For love has 'substance' only in so far as it continually manifests itself in action, in the actual being of the lovers. Thus, even as Benedick empties his word of its content, he denies himself the power to manifest what he feels and intends, and so to make Beatrice experience his love:

BENEDICK: Tarry, sweet Beatrice.
BEATRICE: I am gone though I am here. There is no love in you. Nay, I pray you let me go.
BENEDICK: We'll be friends first.

But a bond is manifested by what it can stand against and by the actions it will beget:

BEATRICE: You dare easier be friends with me than fight with mine enemy.
BENEDICK: Is Claudio thine enemy?
BEATRICE: Is he not approved in the height a villain that hath slandered, scorned, dishonoured my kinswoman? Oh that I were a man! What, bear her in hand until they come to take hands,* and then, with public accusation, uncovered slander, uninstigated rancour – Oh, God, that I were a man! I would eat his heart in the market place.
BENEDICK: Hear me, Beatrice –

* I.e. in the hand-fast of marriage.

32

But she will not listen and he cannot persuade her. Moreover, he has, himself, become linked with Claudio's treachery; for Claudio's nobility, grace, and honour have revealed themselves to be mere surfaces and forms, even as Benedick's vow seems to be mere words:

> BEATRICE: Princes and Counties! Surely a princely testimony, a goodly Count, . . . Oh, . . . that I had any friend would be a man. . . . *But manhood is melted into courtesies, valour into compliment, and men are only turned to tongue, and trim ones too. He is now as valiant as Hercules that only tells a lie, and swears it.* . . .

Value has become a mere dressing, an empty name, easily come by, since no one is ready to confirm its reality in action. If Benedick really loves Beatrice, then he must prove the substance of his vow:

> BENEDICK: Tarry, good Beatrice. By this hand, I love thee.
> BEATRICE: Use it for my love some other way than swearing by it.*

Now Benedick must confront the meaning of his engagement. In a world of shifting appearances, where what is true is elusive, and to be converted is to see with different eyes, he has entered upon a trust that is absolute, that cannot survive the denial of its claim. No end can be served by disputing the meaning of appearances with Beatrice; she loves Hero and believes in her, and Hero's presumed death is a claim that she must answer. By his engagement to Beatrice, Benedick has become involved in her order of reality. Now he must depend on her word; moreover, he must confirm his own word to her with a deed. Love is his compass.

> BENEDICK: Think you in your soul the Count Claudio hath wronged Hero?
> BEATRICE: Yea, as sure as I have a thought or soul.

* Another play on hand-fast.

In the end, it will be as it must be. The toughness of Beatrice's faith will be more impressive testimony for him than the evidence of Claudio's eyes. And he will be right.

> BENEDICK: Enough, I am engaged, I will challenge him. . . .
> *As you hear of me, so think of me.*

Here the union, which is a double union, is sealed. Love binds their formerly separate lives in a single destiny, and, in the deed of love itself, appearance and reality become one. Here they achieve the plane of romantic action: they are religiously committed within a completely human frame.

It is, moreover, their critically imaginative awareness that has made this achievement possible. Being satirically disengaged, they have been able to dwell imaginatively in many realms, and this imaginative grasp of experience and its possibilities has prepared them beforehand for the seriousness of the romantic venture. Benedick, for example, has been a master of the romantic mode long before he has been conscious of his love:

> BENEDICK: O, she misus'd me past the endurance of a block!
> . . . If her breath were as terrible as her terminations, there were no living near her; she would infect to the north star.
> . . . *Will your Grace command me any service to the world's end? I will go on the slightest errand now to the Antipodes that you can devise to send me on; I will fetch you a toothpicker now from the furthest inch of Asia, bring you a length of Prester John's foot, fetch you a hair of the great Cham's beard, do you any embassage to the Pigmies, rather than hold three words, conference with this harpy.* (II. I)

Here is the romantic quest with a vengeance, albeit as a quest to *avoid* the lady. Moreover, the hyperbole employed by the out-witted Benedick goes far beyond any purpose of merely mocking the romantic ideal of service. There is a frustration in its extremity whose counter-side is devotion. This serves to recall that Benedick has never failed to appreciate Beatrice's graces and that he has early declared to Claudio that were Beatrice not 'possessed with a fury', she would exceed Hero 'as much in beauty as the first of May doth the last of December'.

Indeed, the 'conversion' of Benedick and Beatrice, in one sense, has been simply a reversal of direction, not an adoption of a new order. The religious mode of committed existence has been their mode all the while. Benedick is renowned for both his great valour and his unwavering honour. If Benedick and Beatrice have lacked faith, it has been faith that springs from a single mortal human being, not faith as such. They have not been ignorant, moreover, as Claudio has, of the nature of love's bond. On the contrary, the very basis of their resistance to the notion of human love was their precise knowledge of what was at stake. They knew this in the only way they could: *imaginatively*. What they did not know was that such a religion could be seriously viable when sustained by two people with eyes for each other's frailties. In the end, they have to acknowledge that such a faith can sustain itself. But they do so without the self-delusions, without the postulation of a divine image, upon which Claudio's 'love' depends:

> BENEDICK: . . . And I pray thee now, tell me for which of my bad parts didst thou first fall in love with me?
> BEATRICE: For them all together, which maintained so politic a state of evil that they will not admit any good part to intermingle with them. . . . (v. 2)

Beatrice here aims a superbly self-conscious barb at the illusions of lovers. Benedick not only has bad attributes for which she loves him, but his badness is perfection; it admits no single good element to adulterate its purity. In response to this jibe, Benedick drily observes:

> BENEDICK: Thou and I are too wise to woo peaceably.

Their critical realism gives to the bond that is between them a resilient strength. Wittily, they can face the absurdity of love and its wisdom: that it is between two people, frail and fallible, whom mortality never fails to touch; that precisely in this – that men are born to die, and love is for them creation and renewal – lies its necessity and its grace.

Beatrice and Benedick discover what only the sceptic empowered by imagination and ever open to the possibility of commitment can discover: that love is indeed an idea out of imaginative fiction, but that like all ideals it need not remain merely a potential. The real commitment of two lovers may yield love a substantiality and permanence that no dream can have. In this perception Beatrice and Benedick make their way to a central, commonplace, paradoxical truth: that love, in its reality, is romance.

Benedick and Beatrice have multiple perspectives; they are aware of worlds of being and have the power and the will to embrace them, to render substance to what otherwise would remain mere names. In a marvellous metaphor, this restoration of content to form is a restoration for themselves as well. The sacrament of marriage gives them to themselves: they are Benedick – *benedictus* and Beatrice – *beatus*, the blessed. And, in celebration of this happiness and harmony, Benedick undergoes a final conversion to music:

> BENEDICK: . . . Let's have a dance ere we are married, that we may lighten our own hearts, and our wives' heels.
> LEONATO: We'll have dancing afterward.
> BENEDICK: First, of my word; therefore play, music.
>
> (V. 4)

Benedick and Beatrice are not alone in being imaginative critics of love whose very power to penetrate its absurdities makes them better able to master its meanings. Rosalind in *As You Like It* incorporates something of the twin attitudes of these sceptics – though modified in that she never rejects love – and something of their conversion as well. Whole worlds of the imagination and imaginative experience are open to her. She is witty and she is relentless in her pursuit of the illusions of romantic love:

> ORLANDO: What of my suit? . . .
> ROSALIND: Well, . . . I say I will not have you.
> ORLANDO: Then . . . I die.

ROSALIND: No, faith, . . . Men have died from time to time, and worms have eaten them, but not for love.   (IV. I)

With all the force of her wit she resists the mystification of love. Love is between beings who are mortal and changeable and has, therefore, its compelling human realities:

ROSALIND: Now tell me how long you would have [me] after you have possessed [me].
ORLANDO: Forever and a day.
ROSALIND: Say 'a day' without the 'ever'.

There is a wistfulness, despite the wit, in her answer. She is aware of time and refuses to blink the fact that love is an absolute *in* time and not beyond it. She knows herself better than he does; she is not what she was yesterday before he knew her and will be different tomorrow after they are wed:

ROSALIND: No, no, Orlando. Men are April when they woo, December when they are wed. Maids are May when they are maids, but the sky changes when they are wives. I will be more jealous of thee than a Barbary cock pigeon over his hen, more clamorous than a parrot against rain, more newfangled than an ape, more giddy in my desires than a monkey. I will weep for nothing, like Diana in the fountain, and I will do that when you are disposed to be merry. I will laugh like a hyen, and that when thou art inclined to sleep.

In one crucial respect, Rosalind's perception is even sharper than Benedick's and Beatrice's; for she knows that a 'madness' like love, which the whole world shares, is 'reason'.* She does not resist it:

ROSALIND: O coz, coz, coz, my pretty little coz; that thou didst know how many fathom deep I am in love! But it cannot be sounded: my affection hath an unknown bottom,

---

* ROSALIND: Love is merely a madness, and I tell you deserves as well a dark house and a whip as madmen do. And the reason why they are not so punished and cured is that the lunacy is so ordinary that the whippers are in love too.   (III. 2)

like the Bay of Portugal ... that same wicked bastard of Venus [Cupid] that was begot of thought, conceived of spleen, and born of madness, that blind rascally boy that abuses every one's eyes because his own are out, let him be judge of how deep I am in love. I tell thee, Aliena, I cannot be out of the sight of Orlando. I'll go find a shadow and sigh till he come.

The self-awareness here is unflinching and brilliant. She is conscious of the meaning of love, of her love – its inescapable absurdity, its irresistible grace. She is the physician of her own fever and prescribes the very illness which afflicts her, as her only, her desired cure.

It is not only in her self-awareness that Rosalind has affinities with Benedick and Beatrice, but in the enabling use of imagination, which she shares with them. For the range of her consciousness is almost without limit. When she comes upon extravagant verse praises of her virtues, nailed and carved into the trees of the forest Arden, where she is a total stranger, her response is wonderfully characteristic:

CELIA: But didst thou hear without wondering how thy name should be hanged and carved upon these trees?
ROSALIND: I was seven of the nine days out of the wonder before you came; for look here what I found on a palm tree. I was never so berhymed since Pythagoras' time, that I was an Irish rat, which I can hardly remember.   (III. 2)

Pythagoras was for the Elizabethans the author of a doctrine of the transmigration of souls – that the human soul after death passes into the body of an animal. Rosalind chooses an Irish rat for her whimsical metamorphosis, because it was believed that in Ireland rats could be destroyed by incantation in rhyme. The total image she conjures up superbly captures her double astonishment, that the trees of a forest to which she has never ventured should sing forth her name, and in such profuse and extravagant praise.

Rosalind, thus, is like Benedick and Beatrice in the multiple character of her perspective, its inclusion of both the satiric and the romantic attitudes, its imaginative grasp of a whole range of realities. Benedick, Beatrice, and Rosalind are, of course, but three of a gallery of Shakespearean figures who have this redeeming power, 'a multiplied awareness, fantastic imaginations that stretch the whole length of time, place and worlds of the mind' (Chiappe). One who most succinctly typifies the active mode of this awareness and attitude is Bottom the Weaver (his appropriate trade) in *A Midsummer Night's Dream*:

> Bottom is the only figure who can move into the world of fairies, and his imagination is masterful. He is completely at home there, as we are in the theatre. He behaves like a fairy: 'Kill me a . . . humble-bee . . . and bring me the honey-bag.' In the most innocent of human beings there is the power of creation. He wants to take on shows and shadows. He wants to take on every part. He not only creates all parts, but he is his own most effective audience.
>
> (Chiappe)

Bottom's link to the stage serves as a reminder of how over and over again in these plays the metaphor of acting makes its way significantly to the surface. People are always enacting themselves the full range of their selves' possibilities, and realizing themselves in action. In personating a mad Hamlet, Hamlet is in fact personating a chaos of his inner self. It both is and is not Hamlet. What separates Hamlet from Lear in respect of his 'madness' is precisely this power of imagination, the ability to grasp, at once, his own image and, with it, the tension that is choking him, and to enact his own release.

But it is not necessary to single out crisis experience to confirm the metaphor. The enactment of roles, of one's own *personae*, is the mode of human realization, of human *being* and, as such, renders the world a stage. *Active* life *is* drama, and by this very fact graspable in dramatic images. Hence Hamlet, Rosalind, Benedick, and Beatrice have not only large vocabularies of images but large vocabularies of experience as well. In a word, their world of

39

vision is large, and with it their realm of action. They are in-
clusive human beings and share graces with other Shakespearean
characters who, in Viola's phrase, 'can speak in many sorts of
music'.

II. NEW HEAVEN AND NEW EARTH

Human existence is not enacted on a timeless stage, but in a
mutable world, where time alters the appearance of all and,
therefore, where, in order to attain the coherence and substance of
an identity, an imaginative realization must be rooted in something more than the particularity of things and the changeable
wills that fasten on them. It must shape itself along lines that
withstand the shifts of time, and it must accord with commitments and values that remain firm; for it is their constancy, their
failure to dissolve and vaporize, that distinguishes imagined life-
shapes from real.

Just such a tension between imagination and reality underpins
the tragedy of the imperial lovers Antony and Cleopatra, a couple
who realize in their beings something like the fullness of human
potential. It is this very fullness, moreover, that brings them to
crisis. For too rich a realization is its own dissolution. Not only
time undermines it, but its very plenitude denies it concreteness
and the reality that belongs to concreteness:

ANTONY: Eros, thou yet behold'st me?
EROS: Ay, noble lord.
ANTONY: Sometime we see a cloud that's dragonish,
　　A vapour sometime, like a bear, or lion, . . .
　　A forked mountain, or blue promontory
　　With trees upon't, that nod unto the world,
　　And mock our eyes with air. Thou hast seen these signs . . .
EROS: Ay, my lord.
ANTONY: That which is now a horse, even with a thought
　　The rack dislimns, and makes it indistinct
　　As water is in water. . . .

My good knave Eros, now thy captain is
Even such a body: here I am Antony,
Yet cannot hold this visible shape, . . .   (IV. 14)

The tragedy of the lovers is set against the large confrontation
between Rome and Egypt, between the life-conceptions that
these names embody, and it draws major energies from this conflict. Rome is the centre of empire, its life-mode dictated by its
function; in the rough Roman speech of Caesar there is no
lingering moment, no loss of activity in language itself, but a
coursing like the contentious Tiber, an impressment of words, a
forced expression as though the business of politics and history
could not wait upon the clarity of a less clipped address:

CAESAR: . . . the ebb'd man, ne'er lov'd till ne'er worth love,
          Comes dear'd by being lack'd.   (I. 4)

In similar accents, he breaks up the feast on Pompey's ship:

CAESAR: Pompey, good-night. Good brother
          Let me request you off: our graver business
          Frowns at this levity . . .
          . . . the wild disguise hath almost
          Antick'd us all. What needs more words? Good night.
                                                      (II. 7)

In contrast to this Roman usage, language in Egypt is no mere
instrument, but a music, lyrical, fertile, and ambivalent:

CLEOPATRA: O my oblivion is a very Antony
          And I am all forgotten.   (I. 3)

Here it cannot be determined whether the name 'Antony' is invoked as a measure of greatness over-reaching all bounds, or as
the quality of this particular oblivion – an Antonian perfidy equal
in indifference to his attitude towards his wife Fulvia – or whether
the name simply names that oblivion itself, for the consciousness
which she conceives to have expelled her is Antony.

Like its Roman counterpart, the music of Egypt recalls the cadence of its river, overflowing the end of its line, like the spill of the overflowing Nile (Chiappe):

> CLEOPATRA: As sweet as balm, as soft as air, as gentle.
> O Antony ...   (v. 2)

She is speaking of death, of the asp sucking her breast, the 'baby' which is bringing her to Antony, no longer the 'triple pillar of the world' but now simply 'husband', she herself by this deed no longer 'queen', but wife; this death is a meeting, and this dissolution a transformation. It is the paradoxical movement of Old Nilus itself, which brings in its overflow famine and death, and transforms Egypt into a fertile, life-giving ground.

'Overflowing' is more than just a music in this play. As an abundance, an over-bounding flood of energies, it gathers up many of the meanings that cling to 'Egypt' in the play's main confrontation and conflict:

> PHILO: Nay, but this dotage of our general's [Antony]
> O'erflows the measure: ...   (I. 1)

'Nay', 'measure', these are Roman words. Roman measure is a constricting limit which prevents men from pawning 'their experience to their present pleasure'. Confined to proper measure, ruled by judgement, Romans are fashioned into tempered instruments of policy and empire. Discipline, duty, control, stones and monuments, statues rather than 'breathers', these are the Roman ideals. Thus Caesar's praise of Antony's Roman past:

> CAESAR: Thou didst drink
> The stale of horses, and the gilded puddle
> Which beasts would cough at: thy palate then did deign
> The roughest berry on the rudest hedge;
> Yea, like the stag, when snow the pasture sheets,
> The barks of trees thou browsed. On the Alps
> It is reported thou didst eat strange flesh

Which some did die to look on: and all this. . . .
Was borne so like a soldier, that thy cheek
So much as lank'd not.   (I. 4)

A Roman feast. Not the celebration of human company and life's
fruition, but a test of human mettle.

The theme of measure is taken up by the lovers in their first
words:

CLEOPATRA: If it be love indeed, tell me how much.
ANTONY: There's beggary in the love that can be reckon'd.
CLEOPATRA: I'll set a bourn how far to be belov'd.
ANTONY: Then must thou needs find out new heaven, new
    earth.   (I. 1)

Already their love announces itself as so large that it aspires
beyond all existent measures, requires new scales, a transvaluation
of values, to find its adequate frame. Indeed, these figures themselves are so large that they become for each other the measure of
greatness beyond measure, the gauge against which all gradients
must be gauged, the 'odds' of all compare.

Thus, when Antony dies, for Cleopatra it is 'the crown o' the
earth' which melts; gone is the measure and topmost garland of
all human enterprises, which is: to be an Antony –

CLEOPATRA: . . . young boys and girls
    Are level now with men: the odds is gone,
    And there is nothing left remarkable
    Beneath the visiting moon.   (IV. 15)

Antony is not only the greatness of all measure, hence measure
itself, but unlike Roman measures, this 'Antony' is not a limit; it
is a measure which continually surpasses itself:

CLEOPATRA: For his bounty
    There was no winter in 't: an Antony it was
    That grew the more by reaping: . . .   (V. 2)

This is an Egyptian magnitude, quite beyond the limits of Roman possibilities and imagination:

> CLEOPATRA: Think you there was, or might be such a man
> As this I dreamt of?
> DOLABELLA: Gentle madam, no.

But this Roman denial can only be taken as a confession of self-limitation, because such a man has been visibly present only a short while earlier, rewarding his own Judas, Enobarbus, not with thirty pieces of silver, but with a whole treasure, not with animosity and hatred, but with a bounty of compassion and goodwill. Enobarbus himself acknowledges this grace:

> O Antony,
> Thou mine of bounty . . .   (IV. 6)

To recognize the real presence of this Antony who corresponds to Cleopatra's image is of special importance; for such a recognition begins to define the relation between romance and reality which is so central to this play and to the figures who dominate it.

Cleopatra's description of Antony as the measure of all values ('the odds is gone') is of course fundamental romantic hyperbole. It reaches towards hyperbole in its tendency to totalize and universalize its statement as an objective proposition holding outside the romantic relation; but within the relation of love it is simple truth: all movement is either from or towards the other ('it is not as though nothing else were, but all else lives in his light' – Buber). The special reality of *Antony and Cleopatra* is such, however, that the romantic hyperbole *itself* (the totalization of love's value) approaches the status of an objective truth.

Thus, these lovers are praised as 'extravagantly' by outsiders as they are by each other. Antony is not a private illusion cultivated by Cleopatra (Chiappe), nor is Cleopatra an illusion of Antony's. They are in and of the world, which, in a very literal sense, they dominate; they are 'royal' to others, not only to each other, and to hazard the world for love would be no idle metaphor for them.

44

In accord with their archetypal constructions, Antony and Cleopatra share traits in all essential respects with the Shakespearean figures whom we have been considering. In no small way, they represent the fruition of this tradition. They are witty and they are aware, their wit providing their awareness with a potential for comedy which is a fundamental aspect of any self-cognizant attitude. Wit here empowers a self-regarding dimension of the spirit, a disengagement begetting perception and with it the possibility of self-creation, which reaches supreme heights in Cleopatra. Her description of Antony's delights as 'dolphin-like' showing 'his back above the element he lived in' applies to herself. She is superbly aware of herself ('since my lord is Antony again, I will be Cleopatra'), of herself as actress and strategist:

CLEOPATRA: That time? O times!
  I laugh'd him out of patience; and that night
  I laugh'd him into patience, . . .   (II. 5)

          If you find him sad,
  Say I am dancing; if in mirth, report
  That I am sudden sick. . . .   (I. 3)

She uses this self-consciousness, like Falstaff, to outplay herself,* to surpass herself, dolphin-like. Yet the fertility of imagination is so much a mode of her being that it is never merely play:

ANTONY: She is cunning past man's thought.
ENOBARBUS: . . . We cannot call her winds and waters sighs and tears; they are greater storms and tempests than almanacs can report. This cannot be cunning in her; if it be, she makes a shower of rain as well as Jove.   (I. 2)

The fertility of imagination is like the fertility of nature and, indeed, is likened to it by Cleopatra:

          . . . to imagine
  An Antony were nature's piece, 'gainst fancy,
  Condemning shadows quite.   (V. 2)

* As in the second scene with the messenger (III. 3).

45

The same parallel is invoked in Enobarbus' description of her:

> ENOBARBUS: ... she did lie
>   In her pavilion – cloth of gold, of tissue –
>   O'er-picturing that Venus where we see
>   The fancy outwork nature.   (II. 2)

Cleopatra's art *is* nature, breeding her endlessly:

> ENOBARBUS: Age cannot wither her, nor custom stale
>   Her infinite variety: other women cloy
>   The appetites they feed, but she makes hungry,
>   Where most she satisfies.

Thus in her continual self-creation, she shares with Antony that Egyptian bounty, growing ever and ever more bountiful. And, of course, the way in which they 'grow' together under the main reaping movement of time and fortune in this play is the triumphant theme of their tragedy.

Antony and Cleopatra are romantics ('Eternity was in our lips, and eyes, | Bliss in our brows' bent; none our parts so poor, | But was a race of heaven, ...') but they are romantics of a very special ground. For they are no longer young ('grey do something mingle with our younger brown') and they are not naïve about time. If 'eternity' is this present day for them, as romantics, it is not because they are incapable of thinking about tomorrow. On the contrary, it is because they know what tomorrow is; they have lived fully in its shadow. And in the special grace of this play, which is to draw such metaphors to life, they live through the dawn of 'tomorrow' together:

> ANTONY: I am dying, Egypt, dying; only
>   I here importune death awhile, until
>   Of many thousand kisses, the poor last
>   I lay upon thy lips.   (IV. 15)

There is a touching, supremely mature sensualism in the ebbing Antony's 'poor' last. It provides moreover an important measure of the distance between these lovers and those youthful romantics for whom a principal image and desire is 'to die upon a kiss'. For youth, which knows little more than its present hour, may indeed regard the act that seals the future in the present as consummation. But Antony and Cleopatra have lived full lives before meeting. They know what passage means. They have loved life as presence, a field of infinite possibilities. They have loved each other in the shadow of death, knowing that death will finish the feast of their mutual celebration. And it is in this spirit that Antony importunes death awhile, despite the 'many thousand kisses' he has had, to give him time for his 'poor last'.

It is not only in regard to time that their experience provides the ground of their romance, but in regard to the world and their roots in the world as well. They have loved before; Antony is married and Cleopatra has borne children. Moreover, they are both public figures, deeply involved in politics and rule. It is the fact of this involvement which underlies the tension within their relationship, and it is the reality of this tension which Cleopatra will not let Antony blanch:

ATTENDANT: News, my good lord, from Rome.
ANTONY: Grates me, the sum.
CLEOPATRA: Nay, hear them, Antony: . . .   (I. I)

She will not permit him the grand but easy gesture of this half-way dismissal. The news is not trivia to him; if it were, he would not be Antony, a triumvir, 'the triple pillar of the world', dividing its rule with Lepidus and Caesar. It is this *persona* which she recalls for him, by invoking her own:

CLEOPATRA: As I am Egypt's queen,
    Thou blushest, Antony, and that blood of thine
    Is Caesar's homager: . . .

Her invocation of her own royal lineage is also a recall of the fact that his role as triumvir is no negligible one from the point of view of their love. For it is only by virtue of this role and the conquests which led to it, that he could possibly have become worthy

47

to be the lover of Cleopatra, 'Royal Egypt' beloved by Pompey and Julius Caesar before him, the greatest men of their times.

Characteristically, she does more than merely remind him of realities; she provokes him. She is helped to this, and to her own trenchancy, by the possibility that the Roman news may be from Antony's wife, Fulvia (and here history has given to the political tension in their lives a sexual element):

> CLEOPATRA: Fulvia perchance is angry; . . .
> . . . The messengers!
> ANTONY: Let Rome in Tiber melt, and the wide arch
> Of the rang'd empire fall! Here is my space,
> Kingdoms are clay: our dungy earth alike
> Feeds beast as man; the nobleness of life
> Is to do thus: [embracing her]

This is no longer the half gesture of the moment before. Here is the full romantic vision, based moreover on a thorough-going, if un-self-critical, scepticism: the fact of dung, from which politics cannot redeem man, leaves love the sole nobility. It is a measure of Antony that he will not retreat into the compromise towards which she (in the name of 'realism') is urging him; to his romanticism, a love compromised – even with the whole world – is no longer love. It is a measure of Cleopatra's wisdom, however, that she rejects his gesture:

> ANTONY: . . . the nobleness of life
> Is to do thus: when such a mutual pair
> And such a twain can do 't, in which I bind,
> On pain of punishment, the world to weet
> We stand up peerless.
> CLEOPATRA: Excellent falsehood!

Her ambiguous epithet is perfect for his superb but self-undermining statement (for 'such a twain' implies a peerlessness in life as well as love) and she follows this thrust with another:

> CLEOPATRA: Why did he marry Fulvia, and not love her?
> I'll seem the fool I am not; Antony
> Will be himself.

There is a cluster of ironies here which serves to capture the main double tension of their relation. For the first sense of Cleopatra's words is that Antony's marriage proves the reality of his attachment to another world (and to another woman) hence the vacuity of his gesture. A second apparently contradictory, but in fact reinforcing, implication is that Antony has been false to Fulvia and to his own word of love and, therefore, what he says now cannot be taken at face value. The third sense (perhaps just a gleaning) is only comprehensible in its Roman context, where marriage is arranged with an eye to policy and power, not love. In this context, the answer to the question 'why did he marry Fulvia, and not love her' is: for the same reason that he later marries Octavia without loving her, i.e. to shore up a political position. Antony's commitment to the Roman world is a commitment to a world in which politics takes precedence over love.

This tension between them is not, it should be stressed, a tension in the simple sense between their love and a world external to their love which they can easily reject. On the contrary. They love power also. The world will not be well lost by them: they will want to hold it. For 'the world is seen by them to be a part of each other's characters. It is what engages them with each other' (Chiappe); she is 'Egypt' to him and he 'the demi-Atlas of the earth' to her. It is only in so far as the world of politics, of Rome, involves values antithetical to the values of Egypt, particularly love and bounty, that this conflict threatens to break through and become external. But even then it is prevented from doing so by the fact that it is a conflict *within* Antony, between his Roman and Egyptian wills.

There is yet another source of tension in their relation, one stemming from the fact that they are, as Antony says, 'a *mutual* pair', not only tuned to each other, but loving as equals. They are both world rulers and have loved others in their own right. Their commitment to each other is thus not one of dependency or ulterior aim, but is love itself. Their very independence, however, creates a tension as it gives rise to the possibility that they will withdraw into their separate independencies, in a word, that the faith between them will prove to be an insubstantial illusion, and dissolve.

These tensions which beset their relation, tensions of worlds and of faith, are archetypal tensions of love, and their development and resolution is the motive force of the tragedy.

As we have seen, Antony is provoked by Cleopatra into dismissing Caesar's embassy and declaring kingdoms to be mere clay. This action, among others of similar nature, leads to his quarrel with Caesar, his marriage to Caesar's sister Octavia as a means of patching over the quarrel, and therefore to even greater tensions with Cleopatra. Cleopatra is thus correct in recognizing that no commitment to love and Egypt can be absolute for Antony's Roman will, that his gesture of dismissal is mere romance. Indeed, in the very next scene, upon hearing that Fulvia has been making wars against Caesar and that there are actions being launched against him on the fringes of the empire, Antony concludes:

> ANTONY: These strong Egyptian fetters I must break,
> Or lose myself in dotage.   (I. 2)

and he leaves for the desiccated atmosphere of Rome, whose dearth of life, however, cannot engage him for long.

When Antony comes to tell Cleopatra that he is going to Rome, she stops him before he can speak:

> CLEOPATRA: What, says the married woman you may go?
> Would she had never given you leave to come.
> Let her not say 'tis I that keep you here.
> I have no power upon you; hers you are.   (I. 3)

Cleopatra knows that this is not so, that it is her power which keeps him in Egypt, and indeed this is precisely why she experiences such anguish at the prospect of his departure. Thus, without any regard for its contradictory premise, she immediately lays bare the source of her pain:

> CLEOPATRA: Why should I think you can be mine and true
> (Though you in swearing shake the throned gods)
> Who have been false to Fulvia? Riotous madness,

To be entangled with those mouth-made vows,
Which break themselves in swearing!

Thus we return to the central problem of love: how to give substance to the word? The answer, the only answer possible within
the context of this play and these lives is: by dying for it. Only
such a binding can be absolute for them. It is only his death for her,
in the end, that makes him her husband, and her death for him
that makes her his wife. But they do not come to this point
simply; rather, the complex course of their lives gathers up in its
flood the complex meanings of their existence and carries them
towards a final consummation.

The climactic sequence of events begins when Caesar declares
war on Cleopatra and she decides to be present in the battle.
Enobarbus warns her against this:

> ENOBARBUS: Your presence needs must puzzle Antony,
> Take from his heart, take from his brain, from 's time,
> What should not be spar'd. He is already
> Traduc'd for levity, and 'tis said in Rome
> That Photinus, an eunuch, and your maids
> Manage this war. (III. 7)

As Enobarbus' words make clear, Cleopatra's honour, the integrity of her influence on Antony, is at stake. She answers his
warning by saying that since the war is made against her (in a
twofold sense) she will appear. The main motives of their lives are
entangled in the issue of this action.

> CLEOPATRA: Sink Rome, and their tongues rot
> That speak against us. A charge we bear i' the war,
> And as president of my kingdom will
> Appear there for a man. . . .
> I will not stay behind.

Antony also plays a key role in preparing the disaster that follows.
He chooses to fight first by sea, where he is weak, and forgo his
advantage on land, where, as Enobarbus says, he has 'absolute
soldiership'; thus he gives himself up to 'chance and hazard, from

firm security'. Again, the decision that is taken, is taken in accord with the inner contours of their beings:

ANTONY: . . . Canidius, we
  Will fight with him by sea.
CLEOPATRA: By sea, what else?
CANIDIUS: Why will my lord do so?
ANTONY: For that he dares us to 't.

He will fight by sea because he has been challenged to it. Here he manifests the largeness of spirit that makes him Antony ('A rarer spirit never did steer humanity' – Agrippa) and that distinguishes him absolutely from the calculating, politic Caesar, whom he has already dared, in vain, to single fight and to wage the battle on the same ground where Julius Caesar fought Pompey. For Caesar disdains these offers 'which serve not for his vantage'. Antony's romance – to invest the battle with historic meaning, and to make it really a test of value – is futile because the political world is corrupt beyond the redemptive power of the romantic impulse; Caesar merely uses Antony's nobility against him.

In the midst of the ensuing sea battle, a frightened Cleopatra suddenly 'hoists sails, and flies' and 'the noble ruin of her magic, Antony . . . (like a doting mallard) leaving the fight in heighth, flies after her'. Presented with this example and 'instruction', the fleet follows them and the 'Antoniad' is routed.

It has been penetratingly observed that 'Antony's incapacity to be inferior to himself is part of the tragedy' (Zito), and nowhere is that clearer than in these events. From this ebb, though he rallies to show promise of reversal, his fortunes never recover. His final defeat, however, is not directly the result of this disaster in a military sense; indeed, Antony has counted on the possibility of recouping losses at sea in the second engagement on land:

ANTONY: Our overplus of shipping will we burn,
    And, with the rest full-mann'd, from the head of Actium
    Beat the approaching Caesar. But if we fail,
    We then can do 't at land.

What Antony fails to foresee and what really defeats him is the betrayal of his allies and trusted Romans, Enobarbus among them. It is these desertions which sap his strength beyond recall, not – as his Roman critics suggest – Cleopatra. To be sure, Antony's devotion, to a fault, gives a seeming motive to these traitors, but a leader's lapse in judgement does not justify treason, which in the end is based on calculating self-interest.*

It is in the context first of his sea-loss and shame ('I have fled myself and instructed cowards to run, . . .') and then of the betrayal of his generals and final defeat that Antony confronts Cleopatra in a sequence of essential meetings:

> ANTONY: O, whither hast thou led me, Egypt? See,
> How I convey my shame out of thine eyes
> By looking back what I have left behind
> 'Stroy'd in dishonour.
> CLEOPATRA: O my lord, my lord.
> Forgive my fearful sails! I little thought
> You would have follow'd.   (III. 11)

These are the most naked words that Cleopatra has uttered. Disaster has swept her from her throne of complex modes and meanings and given her the need and the power to speak from the heart as though she were a simple maid. Antony responds in similar voice and the exchange between them in their hour of weakness approaches a new level of communication, and even more, of communion:

> ANTONY: Egypt, thou knew'st too well,
> My heart was to thy rudder tied by the strings,
> And thou should'st tow me after. O'er my spirit

---

* The point is made, appropriately by Enobarbus: 'Mine honesty and I, begin to square' he says before leaving Antony. The voice of his self-interest tells him: 'The loyalty well held to fools does make | Our faith mere folly', the voice of his honesty: 'he that can endure | To follow with allegiance a fall'n lord, | Does conquer him that did his master conquer, | And earns a place i' the story.' When Antony learns of Enobarbus' treason, he says: 'O, my *fortunes* have | Corrupted honest men. . . .'

Thy full supremacy thou knew'st, and that
Thy beck might from the bidding of the gods
Command me.

CLEOPATRA: O, my pardon!

ANTONY: Now I must
To the young man send humble treaties, dodge
And palter in the shifts of lowness, who
With half the bulk o' the world play'd as I pleased,
Making and marring fortunes. You did know
How much you were my conqueror, and that
My sword, made weak by my affection, would
Obey it on all cause.

CLEOPATRA: Pardon, pardon!

ANTONY: Fall not a tear, I say, one of them rates
All that is won and lost: give me a kiss,
Even this repays me. . . .

In this last, there is a return to his earlier vision of 'the nobleness of life' – but with what a difference, coming as it does after he has, in *fact*, and not merely in words, given over the clay of kingdoms for his love. Indeed, this very transformation emphasizes that Cleopatra could not have known before, as he says she did, that his heart was to her rudder tied, that she was his compass. He himself did not know this, as his ambiguous actions, leaving for Rome ('I must from this enchanting queen break off') and marrying Octavia, clearly show. Antony's repetition of the point ('you did know how much you were my conqueror') only serves to underline its character as self-recognition. He has been as surprised by his action as she has. It is the movement of recognition, that from this moment accompanies the ebb of their fortunes, and begins to constitute itself as a counter-flow and, in its own way, a redemption.

Perhaps no single image pictures as beautifully the paradoxical movement of their public decline and private ripening as does Cleopatra's, in the moment when a messenger comes unceremoniously from Caesar to answer Antony's vain entreaties:

CLEOPATRA: What, no more ceremony? See, my women
 Against the blown rose may they stop their nose,
 That kneel'd unto the buds.   (III. 13)

The messenger has come bearing Caesar's rejection of Antony's requests. His armies crippled by the desertions of Canidius and the other kings, Antony has entreated the young man to let him live in Egypt, or at least to 'breathe between the heavens and earth, a private man in Athens'; he also has asked that Cleopatra be allowed to maintain her kingdom for her heirs while paying tribute to Caesar. Caesar has vindictively refused Antony's request, but has granted Cleopatra's on condition that she drives Antony from Egypt 'or take his life there'. Caesar's purpose, having defeated Antony, is to see him betrayed by Cleopatra. His failure in this, who has failed in nothing else that he has attempted, whose very name enthrones omnipotence, is one of the main measures of the triumph implicit in the last movement of the play. But before this triumph, the declining pair have ways to travel towards each other.

When the messenger comes from Caesar to Cleopatra, he seeks to win her in a most inept fashion, operating as he must within the narrow circuit of Roman conceptions about human behaviour. His appeal to Cleopatra could not be more inappropriately conceived:

THIDIAS: [Caesar] knows that you embrac'd not Antony
 As you did love, but as you fear'd him.
CLEOPATRA: O!

she toys with him—

THIDIAS: The scars upon your honour, therefore, he
 Does pity, as constrained blemishes,
 Not as deserv'd.
CLEOPATRA: He is a god, and knows
 What is most right. Mine honour was not yielded,
 But conquer'd merely.

At length, she allows him grace to kiss her hand. Antony bursts in upon this and falls at once into a tyrannical passion ('Favours? By Jove that thunders!') and orders the messenger to be whipped. His usage of Cleopatra is no less irresponsible and savage:

> ANTONY: You were half-blasted ere I knew you: ha? . . .
>   I found you as a morsel, cold upon
>   Dead Caesar's trencher: nay, you were a fragment
>   Of Gnaeus Pompey's, besides what hotter hours,
>   Unregistered in vulgar fame, you have
>   Luxuriously pick'd out. For I am sure,
>   Though you can guess what temperance should be,
>   You know not what it is.
> CLEOPATRA: Wherefore is this?
> ANTONY: To let a fellow that will take rewards, . . .
>   . . . be familiar with
>   My playfellow, your hand; this kingly seal,
>   And plighter of high hearts! . . .

But obviously such a small cause cannot lie behind his hysteria. In fact, his own failure and the desertions it has caused have begun to prey on him, and he has been further and more potently struck by the fear that she, for whom he hazarded all, will prove as faithless to him in defeat as his followers:

> ANTONY: To flatter Caesar, would you mingle eyes
>   With one that ties his points?
> CLEOPATRA: Not know me yet?

Thus events conspire to put the same essential question on Cleopatra's lips as was on Antony's earlier. And there is the same ambiguity present. They have been so many things to each other and to the world, and their realities have been so multiple and independent, that the very richness and strength of their identities and relations poses problems: what is real to them and binding? what do they value above other values in their richly engaged lives? These are the questions which the pressure of their declining fortunes presses home to them.

ANTONY: Cold-hearted toward me?

CLEOPATRA: Ah, dear, if I be so,
From my cold heart let heaven engender hail,
And poison it in the source, and the first stone
Drop in my neck: as it determines, so
Dissolve my life; . . .

ANTONY: I am satisfied.

The scene moves towards a reconciliation. But it is one that can only be tentative. For the outburst has revealed more the strength of the forces of dissolution operating in the groundwork of their reality, than any staying power against them. The disintegration of Antony's self-awareness, particularly, has only been too apparent.

Having burst in upon Cleopatra and the messenger, and moving forward to have the latter whipped, he exclaims:

ANTONY: Approach there! [i.e. to Cleo.] Ah, you kite!
Now, gods and devils,
Authority melts from me: of late, when I cried 'Ho!'
Like boys unto a muss, kings would start forth,
And cry 'Your will?' Have you no ears?
I am Antony yet.

But this invocation of his identity 'Antony' is utterly misguided. Nothing could be more removed from Antony than this raging tyrant, spending his impotent fury in flaying Caesar's lackey. Antony is moving towards a dissolution of the sense of himself.

In a way that emphasizes the increasing importance of the question of identity, this scene of their 'reconciliation' ends with a clearly unsatisfactory resolution of the problem with which their fortune confronts them.

Having recovered his 'heart', Antony foresees as well a recovery of their fortunes. He will fight Caesar in Alexandria.

ANTONY: Our force by land
Have nobly held, our sever'd navy too
Have knit again, . . .:
There's hope in 't yet.

57

This hope breeds the necessity for a celebration; its fruition will be the re-firing of their dampened spirits; they will mock death with a fullness of life:

> ANTONY:　　　　Come,
>> Let's have one other gaudy night: call to me
>> All my sad captains, fill our bowls once more;
>> Let's mock the midnight bell.

Cleopatra responds to the larger significance of this, replying,

>> 　　　　. . . since my lord
>> Is Antony again, I will be Cleopatra.

But this is just what they cannot be. These opulent identities were based on a fantastic material bounty made possible by fortune's favour. Now they are hitched to a downward motion of the wheel and these roles no longer answer to reality; events are rapidly robbing them of their basis.

The scenes that follow show an ever-widening fissure between form and substance, the noble lustre of Antony and his ebbing material strength: a life-enhancing figure more and more losing the power to sustain itself as a force in the world.

This movement is expressed in one of the most sublime stage images. As Antony banquets with his captains, the watch hears music from under the boards:

> SECOND SOLDIER:　　　　Peace, what noise?
> FIRST SOLDIER:　　　　　　　　List, list!
> SECOND SOLDIER: Hark!
> FIRST SOLDIER:　　　　Music i' the air.
> THIRD SOLDIER:　　　　　　　Under the earth.
> FOURTH SOLDIER: It signs well, does it not?
> THIRD SOLDIER:　　　　　　No.
> FIRST SOLDIER:　　　　　　　　Peace, I say:
>> What should this mean?
> SECOND SOLDIER: 'Tis the god Hercules, whom Antony
>> loved,
>> Now leaves him.　　　　　　　　　　(IV. 3)

58

A ghostly music heralds the passing of his strength – a leaking away of the power which binds an imperial beauty to an imperial reality, and casts a light over the world.

In the dawn which parts them before the battle, Cleopatra arms her lover and, watching him go, marks with poignant emphasis the invisible but unbridgeable chasm between him and himself:

> CLEOPATRA: He goes forth gallantly: that he and Caesar might
> Determine this great war in single fight!
> Then Antony –; but now – Well, on. (IV. 4)

The light of Antony never burns more brightly than in his last brilliant moments, never by contrast dulls the cold shadow of Caesar more. From his camp before Alexandria, Caesar takes the measure of the military situation, notes that within his files there are enough traitors to Antony, alone, 'to fetch him in' and sympathizes: 'Poor Antony.' In the same breath, he unwittingly offers evidence, however, that there are scales of value in which Antony weighs more than his poverty would indicate:

> CAESAR: . . . feast the army; we have store to do 't,
> And they have earn'd the waste. Poor Antony! (IV. 1)

It is the thought of his own surplus that has made Caesar pity Antony. But what is Caesar's use of his bounty? How does he conceive the feast for his victorious army? A 'waste', a needless expenditure, albeit possible and relatively painless for his overplus, and 'earn'd' by his soldiers. The real 'fruits' of victory for him are power and political advantage, the destruction of the enemy, a monumental name – nothing that can be translated into life.

In the very next scene, by way of contrast, Antony opens his own feast with the three or four remaining loyal captains, saying 'Be bounteous at our meal', thus expressing in one word the meaning of harvest: that its yield is realized in feasting; he gives life who lives it to the full.

Indeed, this image of a bounty bestowing itself on life becomes more and more associated with Antony now, more and more the proper image for his deeds. When Enobarbus deserts, and Antony sends his treasure after him ('O Antony, thou mine of bounty'), it is one of Caesar's soldiers who brings the news:

SOLDIER: . . . your emperor
    Continues still a Jove.   (IV. 6)

And the word 'emperor' repeated by Scarus as, against all judgements, Antony's meagre troops rout Caesar's frontline force of traitors, rings with a special grace:

SCARUS: O my brave emperor, this is fought indeed.
                                        (IV. 7)

And triumphed as well; for before the walls of Alexandria, Antony shows the way to celebrate:

ANTONY: . . . you have shown all Hectors.
    Enter the city, clip your wives, your friends,
    Tell them your feats, whilst they with joyful tears
    Wash the congealment from your wounds, and kiss
    The honour'd gashes whole. . . .   (IV. 8)

There is a tremendous mingling of victories here, a gathering of triumphs, reaching its climax and attaining its symbolic realization as Cleopatra enters:

ANTONY: O thou day o' the world,
    Chain mine arm'd neck, leap thou, attire and all,
    Through proof of harness to my heart, and there
    Ride on the pants triumphing!
CLEOPATRA: Lord of lords,
    O infinite virtue, cam'st thou smiling from
    The world's great snare uncaught?

Antony's response to her question is full of that rich oscillating multiple sense of their multiple selves; they come to fruition in

many ways even as in their own beings they have lived through
many life modes:

ANTONY: My nightingale,
   We have beat them to their beds. What, girl, though grey
   Do something mingle with our younger brown, yet ha' we
   A brain that nourishes our nerves, and can
   Get goal for goal of youth. . . .

And this triumph, though in hard military terms small, is made
large by including in itself so many triumphs of the spirit, and
now – under the genius of this 'lord of lords' and his queen, this
soldier and his girl – enters a kind of apotheosis as it marches
through the city walls:

ANTONY: Trumpeters,
   With brazen din blast you the city's ear,
   Make mingle with our rattling tabourines,
   That heaven and earth may strike their sounds together,
   Applauding our approach.

Hyperbole that this is, it is the hyperbole of an already out-
distanced glory, its fruit melting even as it is tasted; where once
such splendour was a substantial music, it is now but the brilliant
echo of a former greatness, and these but the final thrilling sounds
of a rapidly dissolving instrument.

The final battle finds Antony fatally himself, ready to answer
Caesar's challenge, not to seek his own advantage, but willing to
hazard still the already proven perilous sea:

ANTONY: I would they'ld fight i' the fire, or i' the air,
   We'ld fight there too. . . .   (IV. 10)

There was once an Antony, perhaps, who could war thus, but this
very spirit has robbed him of his sword. His sailors, less heroic
than he, will not lose themselves for such a gesture – and they
desert him. Roman policy, niggardly, calculating, and self-interested, is fashioned for power. It is this spirit that Antony's

Egyptian bounty has betrayed and it is this betrayal that has cost him his forces.

Antony, however, is convinced that the source of his defeat is more concrete; his anguish fuses with his greatest fear and locates it in Cleopatra –

> ANTONY: All is lost:
> This foul Egyptian hath betrayed me:
> My fleet hath yielded to the foe, . . .
> . . . Triple-turn'd whore, 'tis thou
> Hast sold me to this novice, and my heart
> Makes only wars on thee. . . .   (IV. 12)

In his defeat, now absolute and irrevocable, Antony attempts to bind up diverging threads, to see a unity in the chaos of his distress. Cleopatra was the armourer of his heart, the source of his victories in war; now she has begotten his defeat and his heart makes only war on her.

> ANTONY: Betray'd I am.
> O this false soul of Egypt! this grave charm
> Whose eye beck'd forth my wars, and call'd them home;
> Whose bosom was my crownet, my chief end,
> Like a right gipsy, hath, at fast and loose,
> Beguil'd me, to the very heart of loss.
> What Eros, Eros!

> *Enter* Cleopatra

> Ah, thou spell! Avaunt!
> CLEOPATRA: Why is my lord enraged against his love?
> ANTONY: Vanish, . . .

And she does. She is silenced as never before, and communication between them stops. It is in this moment, when his roots into the world are all severed, that Antony experiences the radical dissolution of his identity:

> ANTONY: Eros, thou yet behold'st me?
> . . . here I am Antony,
> Yet cannot hold this visible shape, my knave.

I made these wars for Egypt, and the queen,
Whose heart I thought I had, for she had mine
Which whilst it was mine, had annex'd unto 't
A million more, now lost: she, Eros, has
Pack'd cards with Caesar, and false-play'd my glory
Unto an enemy's triumph.*   (IV. 14)

He has been defined by his relation to Egypt. He has been
'Antony' to her 'Cleopatra', and in this very real sense they have
'beck'd' each other forth. Having betrayed him as he believes she
has, she has robbed him of his sword, and rendered him impotent.
The marriage of meanings implicit in this impotence, the union in
decline of the forces of Mars and Venus, is precisely his conception. He cannot be Antony without her.

The synthesis which Antony achieves in seeing both victory and
defeat as belonging to this grave charm, this soul of Eros, resolves
the conflict between Rome and Egypt. Love has been the spirit
behind his martial victories; betrayed in love, all energies and
hopes exhausted, he is left a Roman, to end simply as a Roman, and
by this stroke to define his relation to himself:

ANTONY: Nay, weep not, gentle Eros, there is left us
Ourselves to end ourselves.

But Antony's synthesis, with its promise of resolution, is far too
simple for this complex world, and violates the sense of what has
happened. Cleopatra's faith did not inspire a sea victory at
Actium, nor was it betrayal by her that caused his defeat. The
moral of Antony's losses, if there is one, is that love and honour
and largeness of spirit are incompatible with military and political
triumph.† This is not a romance world, but a harsh dungy
existence, which a romance world may invade but not encompass.
It is from this larger basis that men must work their meanings out.

Just as Antony reaches his synthetic resolution, Mardian enters

---

* A pun on 'trump'.

† The antithetic character of Mars and Venus is stressed in the play in other
ways, e.g. in the sword imagery: 'She made great Caesar lay his sword to bed' and
Antony's 'My sword, made weak by my affection . . .'

with word of Cleopatra's death, indicating that she has not been in league with Caesar and thus that Antony's synthesis is false. His fortune is a double fortune, turning upon the disparate favours of Mars and Venus, affecting his Egyptian as well as his Roman self.

Word of Cleopatra's death provokes him to this recognition which implies, as a consequence, a new sense of self. To come to this he must strip away his martial trappings:

> ANTONY: Unarm, Eros, the long day's task is done,
> And we must sleep. . . .
> Off, pluck off,
> The seven-fold shield of Ajax cannot keep
> The battery from my heart. . . .
> . . . Apace, Eros, apace!
> No more a soldier: bruised pieces, go,
> You have been nobly borne. . . .

He is moving towards essentials, towards self-discovery, towards re-evaluations:

> ANTONY: I will o'ertake thee, Cleopatra, and
> Weep for my pardon. So it must be, for now
> All length is torture: since the torch is out,
> Lie down and stray no farther. Now all labour
> Mars what it does: yea, very force entangles
> Itself with strength. . . .

This final image, so appropriate for this intricate world (a conflict of positives) looks in two directions. First, in a marvellous way it sums the arc which Antony's tragedy has described – not that of a strong man with a weakness who cracks, but rather a man with two strengths. Second, in its intended emphasis, the image establishes the value that Cleopatra embodies in Antony's world. She is the 'day o' the world'; without her there is no light to light his way.* This romantic image attains a depth here that it has not had before and could not have had. His loss to Caesar, his

---

* Similarly when Antony dies Cleopatra exclaims: 'Ah women, women, | Look, our lamp is spent, it's out. . . .' (IV. 15)

fall from fortune's grace, was an event that could not have
been stayed indefinitely. Antony's constant emphasis on Caesar's
youth is a recognition, however unwilling, of the fact of time's
dominion. The ultimate exhaustion of all energies is a foregone
conclusion, and politics especially belongs to the sublunar world of
mutability and change. What Fortune raises, she brings down;
men cannot ride the top of the wheel forever. And so it has been
with Antony. But something has abided, something transcended
this fall, and that is love. Not a mere sensuality snared in the shifting surfaces of things, but a deeply committed love, constant
before all change, triumphs over time. Death, correspondingly,
ceases to be an exhaustion and becomes – a consummation:

ANTONY: . . . I will be
    A bridegroom in my death, and run into 't
    As to a lover's bed. Come, then; and, Eros,
    Thy master dies thy scholar; . . .

Then, in an ironically accurate moment, Antony bungles his
final Roman gesture which he has (in a further and important
irony) 'learnt of' Eros, who has run on his sword before him. As
he lies dying word comes that Cleopatra is alive in her monument
and that previous report of her death had been false. She had sent
this false report after learning that Antony suspected her of having
'dispos'd with Caesar' and that his rage 'would not be purg'd'.
But 'a prophesying fear' tells her how the stratagem will work
and prompts her to send word again – too late.

It is in the context of this tragedy of errors that their final recognitions come. Cleopatra has a notable celerity of dying, but
Antony believes in the reality of her feigned death this time. He
does so from the same deep mutual intuition that allows Beatrice
and Benedick to know the truth of the deceptions practised on
them. And by the same power of intuition Cleopatra is made to
know that this time her trick will be believed with disastrous
result. She knows that she has his heart; and the image of her
death – which is a 'true' image (for she dies for him later) – tells
him what the events since Actium also have told him: that he has

hers. Something more than their world presence has engaged them with one another, and this bond has abided. It is the bond of a relation in which they are only themselves.

In the final movement of the play it is Cleopatra who dramatizes their pilgrimage through rich and various realizations of identity, to its abiding meaning.

When Antony dies, Cleopatra's world is invaded by vacancy and she swoons. Her waiting-women call to her, their 'sovereign':

CHARMIAN: Lady!
IRAS: Madam! . . .
                                          Royal Egypt:
    Empress!   (IV. 15)

This fanfare of her public identities stirs her, but her speech denies them:

CLEOPATRA: No more but e'en a woman, and commanded
    By such poor passion as the maid that milks,
    And does the meanest chares.

What abides, what in the end has come to dominate the rich chameleon quality of her existence, her majesty of being, what has come to be its meaning – is Antony and her passion for him, a passion which is not hers as Empress, but as a woman.

And her loss, like Antony's, is also a recovery of something like a primal sense of self. Undeniably, a main movement here is rebirth; they are born to each other and to themselves, even as they are dying to the world:

CLEOPATRA: My desolation does begin to make
    A better life: 'tis paltry to be Caesar:
    Not being Fortune, he's but Fortune's knave,
    A minister of her will: and it is great
    To do that thing that ends all other deeds,
    Which shackles accidents, and bolts up change;
    Which sleeps, and never palates more the dung,
    The beggar's nurse and Caesar's.   (V. 2)

Kingdoms are clay. Caesar feeds on the same dung as beggars do; he rides Fortune's wheel, but cannot master it: he serves only mutability and change. From Cleopatra's lips comes the great romantic vision, deliberate in its echo of an earlier Antony. But the vision has been earned now. They have had Fortune peel surfaces from them and disclose the true abiding substance underneath.

There appears, however, to be a radical divergence in Cleopatra's vision here when compared with Antony's earlier. It is not love, in her vision, which transcends time, 'shackles accidents, . . . bolts up change' and liberates from Fortune's wheel – but death. This difference, however, is only apparent; to see the unity, it is necessary to apprehend both the concrete meaning of this particular death, and the complex nature of death itself, when viewed in the play's spectrum.

Over and over in this play we are made to see death as something else than simple negation, and negation itself as more than mere loss. Time is a succession of deaths and negations, and only by being so does it become the plane of realization of all positives, of life. The realization of energies is their expenditure; the very ripening of the fruit prepares its fall. Thus, Cleopatra describes herself as one who is 'with Phoebus' amorous pinches black and wrinkled deep in time'. She is grown old with loving; death (time) is her lover; she expends energies of life and this emptying is her fullness.

The quality that transforms time into triumphs and converts poured-out energies into life-fruitions, is the quality associated in this play with the Nile. Its overflow presages famine and destruction. Yet 'the higher Nilus swells, the more it promises'. 'As it ebbs, the seedsman upon the slime and ooze scatters his grain and shortly comes to harvest.' The same sun, which commits such loving acts upon Cleopatra, breeds life out of the slime from Nilus' overflow. The Nile does not engender fertility by keeping the measure or holding to the mean, but by *overflowing* it. This overflow is also a loss and a destruction, and in this way exemplifies the necessarily ambiguous character of creation.

This Nile fecundity, the power that can transform famine into feasts, is Cleopatra's special grace: 'Vilest things become themselves in her [so] that the holy priests bless her when she is riggish.' A grace transforming. She makes 'defect perfection',* a perfection realized by defect, a perfection that is the perfection of life itself, realized only by a renewable loss, and made to flower only by the continual fall of its fruit.

This fluidity, continual change and renewal, is antithetic to the Roman principle of realization, which is to fashion living energies into monuments of stone. 'Caesar' is one such graven image, a public figure and instrument of power, within which is confined a man. The Romans are static. They do not ripen, and their strength does not go into heaviness. But they are constant. They are true to their own values, and the great Roman gesture – suicide – is the measure of this truth. It is also the measure to which Cleopatra rises in her final act and transfiguration.

She, who has been endlessly various and changeable, dedicates herself, in the end, to a constancy and truth which confirms itself in self-chosen death:

CLEOPATRA: . . . what's brave, what's noble,
     Let's do it after the high Roman fashion,
     And make death proud to take us.   (IV. 15)

This Roman constancy, however, has for her an Egyptian source, and an Egyptian meaning:

CLEOPATRA: Give me my robe, put on my crown. I have
     Immortal longings in me.   (V. 2)

This has generally been understood to mean 'longings for immortality'. But an obviously stronger sense is the literal one. She has immortal longings, longings for Antony that will not die and

---

* ENOBARBUS: I saw her once
     Hop forty paces through the public street
     And having lost her breath, she spoke, and panted,
     That she did make defect perfection,
     And, breathless, power breathe forth.   (II. 2)

68

which she will die to fulfil: death is a meeting and a consummation.

> CLEOPATRA: Show me, my women, like a queen: go fetch
> My best attires, I am again for Cydnus,
> To meet Mark Antony. . . .

The drama of her going is Cleopatra's finest passion, worthy of an art which has been so intimately joined to her life meanings. She will relive their first meeting. The fullness of her death will embody the fullness of her life, a lived fullness, a passionate overflow of imaginatively fecund life energies.

> CLEOPATRA: Now no more
> The juice of Egypt's grape shall moist this lip.
> Yare, yare, good Iras; quick: methinks I hear
> Antony call. I see him rouse himself
> To praise my noble act. . . .

And suddenly there comes a recognition, the emergence of a new identity, a new sense of the relation between them, and the meaning of the fulfilment of their bond:

> CLEOPATRA: Husband, I come:
> Now to that name, my courage prove my title! . . .

Death confirms her troth.

As she takes the asp to untie the 'knot intrinsicate of life' she imagines herself its mother (perhaps as Antony called her his 'Serpent of Old Nile'):

> CLEOPATRA: Dost thou not see my baby at my breast,
> That sucks the nurse asleep?
> CHARMIAN: O, break, break!
> CLEOPATRA: As sweet as balm, as soft as air, as gentle.
> O Antony! . . .

And dying for her is but a final swoon of sense; her calm in death is the calm of consummation:

> CAESAR: . . . she looks like sleep
> As she would catch another Antony
> In her strong toil of grace.

Once again a crucial image looks out of itself with a fluidity of temporal dimensions. 'In her strong toil', is 'in the labour of her final art', confirming in a ritual of transformed identity and re-realized memory, a value transcending time. But a 'toil' is also a 'net', and so characterizes not merely her final action, but herself, her own engaging, transfiguring, lyrical being.

Indeed, what may be said of these lovers is that they have transformed the world with their presence. When they leave it, as Charmian says, it is a vile world that they leave, not worth the staying in. It has been redeemed from its vileness, ennobled, made non-vile,* only by the grace of their presence, by their own 'nobleness of life'.

* The derivation of noble (*nobile*) from 'non-vile' was standard Elizabethan etymology (see *The Tempest*, ed. Frank Kermode, *The Arden Shakespeare*).

3

Imagination and Redemption

I. IMAGINATION AND CATHARSIS

It is only in the world of imagination that a man can work out the truth of his own tragic suffering.

(Chiappe)

When Cleopatra sends false word to Antony that she is dead, it is because she sees that his 'rage' will not be 'purged'. His rage wills her death. When she leaves in the middle of his fury, he says:

> ANTONY: 'Tis well th'art gone,
>   If it be well to live.   (IV. 12)

and again:

> ANTONY: The witch shall die,
>   To the young Roman boy she hath sold me, and I fall
>   Under this plot: she dies for it. . . .

Possessed by his passion, he speaks of her as if he were a god to punish.* Only the image of her death, the irreparable loss of the thing he loves, can bring him back to reason, to his sense of himself, and Cleopatra, and the bond between them.

These are characteristic moments in the universe of Shakespearean tragedy. Infected with tyrannical passions, men strike like avenging gods against the beings whom they love. So absolute is their domination by these passions that they are, in effect, mad.

---

* The phrase is from *Coriolanus*: 'You speak o' th' people | As if you were a god to punish, not | A man of their infirmity . . .'

They do not 'see' reality, and are incapable of seeing it, until they are purged.

Thus when Lear, acting in 'hideous rashness', pronounces his 'doom' against his youngest and truest daughter Cordelia, wise counsels are of no avail; they will not be heard, their sight will not be tested:

KENT: Good my Liege, –
LEAR: Peace Kent!
    Come not between the Dragon and his wrath. . . .   (I. I)

Lear seeks to silence counsel, as though his judgement were divine (and indeed 'wrath' is the proper anger of divinity) and not open to question. To gain a hearing, Kent therefore stresses his *human* bonds to Lear and, by implication, Lear's own humanity:

KENT: Royal Lear,
    Whom I have ever honour'd as my king,
    Lov'd as my father, as my master follow'd,
    As my great patron thought on in my prayers, –

Lear rebuffs this gesture and affirms the engine-like, abstract nature of the justice pronounced, as though not a personal judgement, but a process of the universe itself had been engaged:

LEAR: The bow is bent and drawn; make from the shaft.

This is megalomaniac. Indeed, Kent implies as much, as he drives home the reality of Lear's human frailty, a frailty that prevents any sentence he may pass from attaining the status of divine doom:

KENT: Let it fall rather, though the fork invade
    The region of my heart: be Kent unmannerly,
    When Lear is mad. What would'st thou do, *old man*? . . .

But Lear will not see the truth. He wills not to see any reality but his own:

LEAR: Out of my sight!

And his way is made for darkness.

The purgation of a passion very like Lear's, and the restoration of its subject to humanity and reason, is a major movement of the late romance, *The Winter's Tale*. Like Lear, King Leontes is possessed by a passion that infects his judgement, deals out dooms that are the province of gods, and remains deaf to the voices of human reason.

There is not an eye in Leontes' court that will bear witness to the adultery which he believes to have transpired between his wife Hermione and his best friend Polixenes, not a voice that will second his belief in this. Yet, the more his judgement is denied by his councillors, the more it is confirmed for him. Nothing can alter his outlook. Not the testament of others, nor the sight of his own eyes will remove the rotten root of his opinion. When Paulina brings Hermione's new-born babe to him in the hope that he may 'soften at the sight o' th' child', and shows him that it is his ('Behold, my lords, although the print be little, the whole matter and copy of the father'), he commands that it be committed to destruction.

Thus, like Lear, Leontes sets his judgement above that of mere humanity. His *hubris* reaches its acme when the oracle of Apollo is read, proclaiming that 'Hermione is chaste; Polixenes blameless; . . . Leontes a jealous tyrant; his innocent babe truly begotten; and the king shall live without an heir if that which is lost be not found.'

LEONTES: Hast thou read truth?
OFFICER: Ay, my lord, even so
   As it is here set down.
LEONTES: There is no truth at all i' th' Oracle: . . .   (III. 2)

Here Leontes reaches the ultimate length to which he can go in imposing his own will upon reality and bending it, tyrannically, to the shape of his passion. Now the great purging shocks begin, the losses which he must sustain before he can find himself again:

SERVANT: My lord the king, the king!
LEONTES: What is the business?

SERVANT: O sir, I shall be hated to report it!
  The prince your son, with mere conceit and fear
  Of the queen's speed, is gone.
LEONTES: How! gone?
SERVANT: Is dead.

And now the great reversal:

LEONTES: Apollo's angry, and the heavens themselves
  Do strike at my injustice. . . .

But the death of Leontes' young son Mamillius only begins his return to reality. Reconciliation with his wife Hermione, recognition of the nature of what he has done, and creation of a new, more adequate self, require a more elaborate purgatorial experience. In particular, reconciliation with Hermione must be prepared by confrontation with the imagined fact of her death, and reconstitution of self can be achieved only through the tempering contemplation of the possibilities of new life that by his hasty deed of doom he has lost.

The partial character of Leontes' initial reversal and hence the necessity for what will become a sixteen-year purgatory is apparent in his contrition at the death of his son. Death is the irreversible deed, the irreparable loss that distinguishes men from gods and makes human frailty and infirmity unfit to judge and doom as Leontes has done. But Leontes' first thoughts are not of those he has cast into oblivion, the innocent babe he has sent to destruction, the child whose heart he has broken, the wife whom he has bereft of his favour, which she accounts more than life. He thinks of himself. He seeks first to square himself with Apollo, whose oracle he has profaned, then with his queen, his friend Polixenes, and his servant Camillo, whom he has sought to corrupt:

LEONTES: . . . how he glisters
  Through my rust! and how his piety
  Does my deeds make the blacker!

It is at this point, when the limits of Leontes' contrition are apparent, that Paulina enters with false word of Hermione's death, saying that she died grieving over her lost children. Paulina bids Leontes think what his tyranny and jealousies have done 'and then run mad indeed: stark mad!' His betrayal of Polixenes 'was nothing', nor was it much to have poisoned Camillo's honour, when compared with his crimes against his family, with which he has yet to reckon. Indeed, Hermione's reported death is but the symbolic realization of her actual condition, because Leontes has bereft her of all reasons for living: her honour, his love, her children, all the comforts of her life. Prompted by a just cause, Leontes' deeds against Hermione (not to mention those against his children) would be wrong and harsh; causeless, they are monstrous:

PAULINA: . . . O thou tyrant!
 Do not repent these things, for they are heavier
 Than all thy woes can stir: therefore betake thee
 To nothing but despair. A thousand knees
 Ten thousand years together, naked, fasting,
 Upon a barren mountain, and still winter
 In storm perpetual, could not move the gods
 To look that way thou wert.

Leontes is moved by this truth. He asks Paulina to bring him to the dead bodies of his queen and son, whom he will have buried in one grave.

LEONTES: Once a day I'll visit
 The chapel where they lie, and tears shed there
 Shall be my recreation. . . .

Leontes' travail, his daily pilgrimage to the grave, and his confrontation there with the image of his deed and loss, recall an earlier Shakespearean moment. In *Much Ado About Nothing*, Friar Francis devises a mock death for Hero, whose purpose he describes in the following terms:

FRIAR: When [Claudio] shall hear she died upon his words,
 The idea of her life shall sweetly creep
 Into his study of imagination, . . .   (IV. I)

The image of the dead Hero, killed by him, will teach him what he has lost; he will learn the bounty he had when she was alive, whose value he had not the sense to appreciate:

FRIAR: ... for so it falls out,
   That what we have we prize not to the worth,
   Whiles we enjoy it; but being rack'd and lost,
   Why, then we rack the value, then we find
   The virtue that possession would not show us
   Whiles it was ours: ...

Thus our sense of what we have is dependent upon our imagination of what it would mean not to have it, our self-sense on comprehending how we destroy what we need. Such a study of imagination not only deepens perception, but prepares the ground of a new 'world' of perception, hence new life:

FRIAR: ... on this travail look for greater birth.

The double knowledge that this study of imagination is designed to bring, self-knowledge and knowledge of what's lost, is also the content of Leontes' exercise. This is apparent in his answer to Cleomenes, when the latter advises him, after sixteen years, to forget his evil and forgive himself, as one having 'paid down more penitence than done trespass'.

LEONTES: Whilst I remember
   Her, and her virtues, I cannot forget
   My blemishes in them, and so still think of
   The wrong I did myself: which was so much
   That heirless it has made my kingdom, and
   Destroy'd the sweet'st companion that e'er man
   Bred his hopes out of.   (v. 1)

'Winter' is the proper season to serve as the main image for this play, for it is the natural image of death, teaching man, in the twofold sense above, what he is:

DUKE: Here [in nature] feel we ...
   The seasons' difference, ... the icy fang

76

And churlish chiding of the winter's wind,
. . . when it bites and blows upon my body,
Even till I shrink with cold, I smile and say
'This is no flattery. These are councillors
That feelingly persuade me what I am. . . .'
                              (*As You Like It*, II. 1)

Knowledge of what man is, of the winter dearth towards which
he is headed, gives him the grace of knowledge of what he has,
and makes him tend the seeds of his fruition. In the image of
winter, man perceives his future, and this perception and its
knowledge serves to make his 'love more strong',

To love that well which [he] must leave ere long.
                              (Sonnet 73)

Thus the comment appended to the speech on winter in *As You
Like It* is appropriate not only to the speaker, but to his meaning:

Happy is your grace,
That can translate the stubbornness of fortune
Into so quiet and so sweet a style.   (II. 1)

And thus, the fruition actually achieved by Leontes' lost child
Perdita and her lover Florizel, is achieved consciously on the edge
of 'summer's death and the birth of trembling winter'.

Leontes' wintry contemplation is more than a mere study,
however. It is a penance, a spiritual exercise that tempers his being,
disciplines his hot summer blood, purges the pitiless spirit that
committed his child to destruction and severed all the lifelines of
his 'gracious' queen, and it looks towards greater birth.

A related if less grave penance is imposed on the courtier
Berowne in *Love's Labour's Lost*, which throws light on the function of the image of death in Leontes' exercise. Berowne is noted
for his caustic and devastating wit; he is 'a man replete with
mocks . . . and wounding flouts' which he 'executes' on all
estates of people who 'lie within the mercy of [his] wit', and it is
of this disposition that he must be 'purged'.

'To weed this wormwood from [his] fruitful brain', he must 'visit the speechless sick' and 'groaning wretches', where his task will be

> With all the fierce endeavour of [his] wit
> To enforce the pained impotent to smile.   (v. 2)

If 'sickly ears' will hear his 'idle scorns', he may continue as he is, but if not, he must 'throw away that spirit' and be reformed.

Berowne protests:

> BEROWNE: To move wild laughter in the throat of death?
> It cannot be; it is impossible:
> Mirth cannot move a soul in agony.

The impossibility is precisely the point of the exercise, which is 'to choke a jibing spirit'. For 'a jest's prosperity lies in the ear of him that hears it, never in the tongue of him that makes it'. The ideal of the comic spirit is something like the ideal contained in Falstaff's remark that he is not only witty in himself, but the cause that wit is in other men – where 'wit' of course means both 'sense' and 'humour'.*

Wit is fecund. It crowns and makes possible life's feast, which is always lived on the brink of trembling winter. A true wit, therefore, is sympathetic not scornful, restorative not wounding. Berowne's fault, like Leontes' – though considerably milder – has been to use people as though he were a god to punish, and not a man of their infirmity. Death, in whose image he can see his own fragile and transparent nature, his 'glassy essence', provides the proper check for this spirit. By impressing him with the brevity of his authority, it teaches him to temper its impact with mercy and grace.

At Hermione's trial, which itself is a savage punishment for her (and only that, for it comes before the oracle's judgement), she reminds the court of this spirit of grace which is absent:

> HERMIONE: The Emperor of Russia was my father:
> O that he were alive, and here beholding

* Particularly as irony, the ability to see on different levels.

His daughter's trial! that he did but see
The flatness of my misery, *yet with eyes*
Of pity, not revenge! (III. 2)

It is Leontes' failure to temper his judgement with the grace of
mercy that causes him to destroy and cast out the seeds of renewal,
thus making a winter not only of his present, but of his future as
well. It is this which Leontes' pilgrimage to the grave teaches him.
In Hermione he has 'destroy'd the sweet'st companion that e'er
man bred his hopes out of'. He is not a god, the source of his own
spring. Hermione's grave is, therefore, his own grave, he cannot
be revived without her.

By a special grace of Shakespeare's art in this play, however, the
lost fruition is allowed to realize itself and to draw forth the
restorative and reconciling powers of a reborn spring.

In the countryside of Bohemia, where shepherds have taken
pity on Hermione's cast-out babe and raised her for sixteen years,
a pastoral celebration is in process. The central figures of this
celebration are Florizel, Polixenes' son, and Perdita, the lost child
of Leontes, whom Florizel loves and now seeks to marry. This
union is the fruition which Leontes has apparently destroyed; it
contains within it the seed of a reunion with Polixenes, and also
the restoration of Leontes' now heirless line in the kingdom of
Sicilia.

However, Polixenes comes to the feast in disguise, fearing that
his son Florizel will throw away his nobility on a 'sheep-hook',
i.e. the unknown child of Leontes, Perdita. When Polixenes and
Camillo arrive at the festival, Perdita gives them flowers, which
are the symbolic flowers of Leontes' state:

PERDITA: Reverend sirs,
   For you there's rosemary, and rue; these keep
   Seeming and savour all the winter long:
   Grace and remembrance . . .   (IV. 4)

They are proper flowers for Polixenes too, whose winter age,
like Lear's, breeds a choleric temper which threatens to destroy

what he loves, and therein himself. When Florizel persists in his intention to marry the 'shepherdess' Perdita, Polixenes discloses himself and cries:

> POLIXENES: Mark your divorce young sir,
> Whom son I dare not call; thou art too base
> To be acknowledged; . . .

Polixenes threatens to kill Perdita's shepherd 'father', scratch her beauty with briers, and bar Florizel from succession should he but sigh over the fact that he shall never see her again. Once more an intervention by the servant Camillo prevents his master's treachery, and the young couple are able to flee to Sicilia, the kingdom of Leontes.

With their arrival, the effect of Leontes' penance is made visible. In this young couple he sees the image of what he has lost by his compassionless vengeance:

> LEONTES: O, alas!
> I lost a couple, that 'twixt heaven and earth
> Might thus have stood, begetting wonder, as
> You, gracious couple, do: . . .   (v. 1)

Polixenes, in hot pursuit of the fleeing lovers, now arrives in Sicilia and sends a messenger to Leontes' court, bidding the king arrest Florizel. Florizel asks Leontes to intercede on his behalf and thus puts him to the test: have the tears shed at Hermione's grave been his re-creation?

> FLORIZEL: Beseech you, sir,
> Remember since you ow'd no more to time
> Than I do now: with thought of such affections,
> Step forth mine advocate: . . .

Florizel appeals to Leontes' compassion, to his remembrance of his own youth when he had like desires and perhaps stood in a similarly helpless position. Leontes' penance has well equipped him to make such a comparison; he has before him the awful contrast of images of himself sixteen years earlier, pitilessly dealing out doom, and then, a moment after, so brought to naught himself that nothing in his power could compel the gods to look on him and show him the mercy he had refused.*

Thus, when Florizel says that Polixenes, at Leontes' request, would 'grant precious things as trifles', Leontes responds generously:

LEONTES: Would he do so, I'd beg your precious mistress,
    Which he counts but a trifle.

There is an ambiguity in the form of Leontes' answer, a fact which Paulina quickly notes, for it implies almost that he would beg Perdita for himself (and, of course, in one of the wonderful ironies of this play he would – because, unknown to all, she is his daughter).

PAULINA: Sir, my liege,
    Your eye hath too much youth in 't; not a month
    'Fore your queen died, she was more worth such gazes
    Than what you look on now.
LEONTES: I thought of her,
    Even as these looks I made. . . .

Leontes sees in Perdita the image of Hermione, of all that he has lost, and it is this remembrance, and its attendant rue,† which moves him to answer Florizel's petition and to intercede with Polixenes for the young couple. Now the 'miracles' of the play unfold, the symbols become realities, come to life: this *image* of his lost child *is* his lost child Perdita; this semblance of his lost wife Hermione, is Hermione's real flesh image, her child; and again, in its wonderful art, the play enacts this theme of realization – the image of Hermione, a statue produced by Paulina, becomes Hermione herself, stirred to life by Leontes' awakened faith and her found child, to be reconciled and reunited with them.

Tears shed at Hermione's grave have indeed been Leontes' re-creation, his grace.

---

* The same situation, making the same point, is central to *Measure for Measure*.
† 'There's rue for you, and here's some for me – we may call it herb of grace o' Sundays' – Ophelia.

Here did she fall a tear; here in this place
I'll set a bank of rue, sour herb of grace.
(*Richard II*, III. 4)

Tears of grief as watering grace,* a fructifying rain, a power of
renewal that calls forth other compassionate powers:

CORDELIA: All bless'd secrets,
 All you unpublish'd virtues of the earth,
 Spring with my tears! Be aidant and remediate
 In the good man's distress! . . .   (IV. 4)

Rue as grace, remorse, a pity for the sufferings one has caused, a
late compassion which earlier would have granted the pardon
(grace) which would have prevented one's own crimes.

Viewed in this way, compassion is a self-preserving force. It is
putting oneself in the place of others, seeing oneself as one of their
infirmity and imagining their sufferings as possible to oneself; it is
the recognition of an essential humanity, despite all apparent
differences, in which one shares:

LEAR: I am a very foolish fond old man . . .   (IV. 7)

The effecting of this recognition, a recognition which includes the
existence of others, which experiences self as a possibility of other
selves, is the function of imagination (significantly, of *theatrical*
imagination); it implies a purgation of senses and passions, a
stripping of appearances, a confrontation with essential identities.
Thus Lear, shut out by his two daughters, stripped of his offices,
honours, and all appurtenances of rule, confronts the naked
Edgar, disguised as Poor Tom o' Bedlam:

LEAR: . . . thou art the thing itself; unaccommodated man is
 no more but such a poor, bare, forked animal as thou art.
 Off, off, you lendings! Come; unbutton here. (III. 4)

Here in physical identification with naked man, Lear finds a
bedrock of his reality. It is a measure of the weakness of his

 * '. . . Grace grow where those drops fall, . . .' – Antony.

imagination that Lear must literally *enact* these recognitions, which prepare his own purgation. Indeed, his own chosen image for this process is 'physic':

LEAR: Take physic, Pomp;
Expose thyself to feel what wretches feel,
That thou mayst shake the superflux to them
And show the Heavens more just.

He must himself be turned out under the 'wrathful skies', experience 'the tyranny of the open night' to learn what 'houseless poverty' is like and the 'poor naked wretches' who have inhabited his kingdom:

LEAR: O! I have ta'en
Too little care of this . . .

The emergence of pity, in the storm, marks the beginning of Lear's regeneration:

LEAR (to the Fool): In, boy; go first. You houseless poverty, –
Nay, get thee in. I'll pray and then I'll sleep.

It is the first time that Lear has thought of another. The development of this new awareness is not regular, but fitful and at the same time revealing and characteristic. When he sees Poor Tom, his wit destroyed and naked in the storm, Lear can comprehend Tom's misery only as a facet of his own; he sees only an image of himself:

LEAR: Didst thou give all to thy daughters?
And art come to this?

The tremendous irony here is that Poor Tom is Edgar, driven out by his father, and hence not Lear's image but Cordelia's. If Lear saw truly, he would see in Edgar his own crime, not a sympathetic suffering.

Once again the voice of Kent breaks in upon him to make him see better:

KENT: He hath no daughters, Sir.
LEAR: Death, traitor! . . .

A re-enactment, a momentary reversal. Lear is groping, but he is
stripped of power and *persona* and sees 'feelingly' now, and there is
no danger that he will remain ignorant of others and of himself.
In the image of the wrongs done him, he begins to grasp the
wrongs done others, done man in general; in the image of
wronged man, he grasps his own image; and then he issues in a
new direction, entirely, grasping the image of the wrongs he has
done* –

> LEAR: Be your tears wet? Yes, faith, I pray weep not.
> If you have poison for me, I will drink it.
> I know you do not love me; for your sisters
> Have, as I do remember, done me wrong:
> You have some cause, they have not.
> CORDELIA: No cause, no cause. . . .
> LEAR: You must bear with me.
> Pray you now, forget and forgive: I am old and foolish.
>
>   (IV. 7)

The regenerative movement out of the tragic abyss, involving
essential recognitions leading to essential reconciliations, is the
central movement of Shakespeare's last romance, *The Tempest*.
Here, in a play which recapitulates many main Shakespearean
moments, the artifice of grace, its nature as art, is a primary
theme.

The actual crime against Prospero precedes the play's action,
which begins with a conjured tragic tempest raining down images
of doom and separation on those who have sinned against him.
The central action of the play is Prospero's imagination of a
purgatory for these sinners, which he bodies forth through the
agency of Ariel, a spirit of the air. Indeed, airs as attitudes, graces,
music – all these meanings converge in the redeeming actions
which take place on Prospero's isle:

> ALONSO: O, it is monstrous, monstrous!
> Methought the billows spoke, and told me of it;

---

* This process is, of course, not a simple progression. He does it over and over,
'bound upon a wheel of fire'.

The winds did sing it to me; and the thunder,
That deep and dreadful organ-pipe, pronounc'd
The name of Prosper: it did bass my trespass.
Therefore my son i' th' ooze is bedded; . . .   (III. 3)

As in *Lear*, the great separations, which the tragic tempest brings
about, provoke those recognitions and self-recognitions that prepare the possibility of reconciliation. Alonso must himself plum-
met to the depths of adversity in order to recognize the meaning
of his crime against Prosper, which was to topple him to similar
desperate estate. In more than one sense it is necessary to be lost in
order that one may be found:

GONZALO: Was Milan thrust from Milan, that his issue
    Should become kings of Naples? O rejoice
    Beyond a common joy! . . . in one voyage
    . . . Ferdinand . . . found a wife
    Where he himself was lost, Prospero his dukedom
    In a poor isle, and all of us ourselves
    When no man was his own.   (V. 1)

Upon the great theme of recognition, celebrated in the romances,
moreover, *The Tempest* makes an important elaboration. For not
all the sinners in this play recognize their guilt as such, despite the
inducements of Prospero's potent art. Antonio and Sebastian, the
most sinning of all, seek to fight the accusing vision (Ariel),
which moves Alonso and the others to their contrition:

SEBASTIAN: But one fiend at a time,
    I'll fight their legions o'er.
ANTONIO: I'll be thy second.   (III. 3)

This failure of vision extends the whole range of the isle and its
possibilities for them:

ADRIAN: [The isle] must needs be of subtle, tender, and
    delicate temperance. . . . The air breathes upon us here most
    sweetly.
SEBASTIAN: As if it had lungs, and rotten ones.
ANTONIO: Or as 'twere perfumed by a fen.

GONZALO: Here is everything advantageous to life.

ANTONIO: True; save means to live. . . .　　　　(II. 1)

The irony is that the isle possesses means not only advantageous to physical life (food in abundance, magic which has rescued them from the storm) but also to the life of the spirit and its renewal. The 'moral' of Antonio's non-redemption and its relation to his failure of vision, has already been invoked by Albany in respect to Goneril:

Wisdom and goodness to the vile seem vile.　　(*Lear*, IV. 2)

There is something in vileness that perpetuates itself, because it has not the imagination to envision the non-vile, the noble, and hence lacks the conceiving power to give it birth.

Another theme of grace which *The Tempest* enlarges upon and, in effect, consummates, is judgement. It is the thunder which basses Alonso's trespass, the instrument of high-judging Jove. This 'dread rattling thunder' is, however, 'given fire' not by Jove, but by Prospero, whose '*rough* magic' makes him the 'god o' the island', but who, nonetheless, is a passionate human being, 'crabbed' by age, and prone to a certain harshness in dealing with those within his power. This harshness is often of the moment, the result of an upsurge of passion, rather than an ingrained attitude. But it is precisely the possibility of this upsurge that makes god-like power, the power of judgement, in human hands so dangerous; for it is in these upsurgent moments that irreparable damage is done. A calculated harshness is often necessary to shatter false consciousness (e.g. Alonso's) or to subdue hardened evil (e.g. Antonio's). But man, 'proud man, dressed in a little brief authority', plays 'fantastic tricks before high Heaven' and uses his thunder to strike at human helplessness, to revenge himself on what has already been subdued, or even to punish the defenceless innocent in whom he 'sees' some imagined tincture or taint.*

* 'Could great men thunder | As Jove himself does, Jove would ne'er be quiet, | For every pelting, petty officer | Would use his Heaven for thunder. | Nothing but thunder! Merciful Heaven, | Thou rather with thy sharp and sulphurous bolt | Split'st the unwedgeable and gnarled oak | Than the soft myrtle.' – *Measure for Measure*.

Thus, the action of *The Tempest* reaches a critical point as Prosper's purgatorial drama approaches its climax, with its subjects all 'confin'd' and 'distracted':

ARIEL: Your charm so strongly works 'em,
That if you now beheld them, your affections
Would become tender.   (V. I)

'Affection' in Shakespearean psychology is the 'master of passion', * presumably, that desire which summons forth corresponding feelings and emotions. Ariel is saying, therefore, that the sight of his victims' suffering will transform Prospero's harsh vengeance-seeking affection, to a tender one seeking reconciliation, something like their restoration or redemption.

PROSPERO: Dost thou think so, spirit?
ARIEL: Mine would, sir, were I human.

The source of the transformation of affections lies in the fact of common humanity, a sense of identity between judge and judged, executioner and victim, and a tenderness springing from it:

PROSPERO: And mine shall.
Hast thou which art but air, a touch, a feeling
Of their afflictions, and shall not myself,
One of their kind, that relish all as sharply
Passion as they, be *kindlier* mov'd than thou art?

Here Prosper names the well-spring of his pardon, which is to follow. It is in his kind-ness, his nature which he shares with them. For he feels afflictions as they do, passions as they (where 'passions' has a verbal emphasis, suggesting 'to experience feelingly') and thus is moved to mercy by the image of himself, suffering in their agony.

This *compassion*, Prospero calls a 'nobler reason' which checks his 'fury' and makes him recognize that 'the rarer action is in virtue than in vengeance'; his subjects being penitent, 'the sole drift' of his purpose does not extend 'a frown further'. Indeed, the

* *Merchant of Venice*, IV. I. 50.

87

tempering of his justice with mercy will underlie the restorations and reconciliations that ensue, and make possible, even for him, a new birth. He will be restored to his dukedom in Milan, 'lose' his daughter to be Ferdinand's wife, and hence 'find' his issue kings of Naples.

Prospero's designation of a passion (i.e. com-passion) as a nobler reason, joins this to an earlier Shakespearean theme, namely, the sense of sense (as in *Hamlet*). To this doubleness of reason there corresponds moreover a doubleness of grace. There is a grace of control, subduing flesh, nurturing nature, refining its savagery and tuning its sense to harmonize with reason; and there is a grace of compassion, an attunement to the passion of others, abandoning vengeance in the face of atonement and for the sake of at-onement,* a grace which tunes the harmony by which men can prosper:

HYMEN

Then is there mirth in Heaven
When earthly things made even
Atone together.
(*As You Like It*, v. 4)

II. ROMANCE† PERSPECTIVES‡ AND POSSIBILITIES

After Alonso is reconciled with Prospero, but before the latter tells him that his son Ferdinand is not drowned, he bemoans his loss as 'irreparable':

ALONSO: . . . patience
Says it is past her cure. (v. 1)

* Atone = at-one, 'to achieve unity or concord'.
† The literary genre.
‡ The word 'perspective' was associated by Shakespeare with perspective pictures, so constructed that 'rightly gaz'd upon, show nothing but confusion; ey'd awry, distinguish form'. It also suggested to him a perspective, or multiplying glass, cut into a number of facets each giving a separate image, thus a glass which 'divides one thing entire to many objects'. And finally, it suggested a perspective or prospective glass, a magic crystal which could be used to look into the distance or future. Cf. *King Richard II*, ed. Peter Ure, *The Arden Shakespeare*, pp. 70–1.

To this, Prospero replies:

> PROSPERO: I rather think
> You have not sought her help, of whose soft grace
> For the like loss I have her sovereign aid,
> And rest myself content.

Prospero, of course, can afford the 'soft grace' of patience because he has only 'lost' a child to marriage; moreover, he knows that Alonso's son is not drowned. That, nonetheless, he is made to stress the moral is a sign of the importance which his creator attached to it. For this is a symbolic drama (derivative of masque forms) and the grace of patience is without question a formidable force in the Shakespearean universe.

In the climactic moment of another late romance, *Pericles*, this power is impressively manifested as Pericles matches his own endurance of grief and injury against Marina's. The contrast between the ruined Prince and the young girl who confronts him is radical indeed. He has lost (or so he thinks) both wife and child, she both father and mother. But while Pericles' losses have led him to withdraw, speechless, from the community of men, Marina has been tempered by adversity, rather than subdued or distorted by it. She is brought to him to cure his 'distemperature', to take him out of his grave.

She sings for him and she speaks of her own trial, of time which has 'rooted out' her parentage. Some glint of recognition ('fortunes and parentage') breaks through his wall of silence. It is the same recognition that Leontes has of lost possibilities; he has found in Marina the image of his lost loves:

> PERICLES: I am great with woe
> And shall deliver weeping. My dearest wife
> Was like this maid, and such a one
> My daughter might have been: . . . (v. i)

She looks, he says finally, 'like Patience gazing on kings' graves and smiling extremity out of act'. There is in Marina a temperament which refuses to be subdued into a vision of all as 'dark and comfortless'. Thus while Pericles' great suffering entombs him, buries him alive, Marina's patience masters her suffering and makes of her a redeeming figure:

PERICLES: O, come hither,
 Thou that beget'st him that did thee beget;

For in the characteristic manner of the late romances, the wonder is made strikingly rare, as Marina herself is revealed to be Pericles' lost daughter, now miraculously found.

It is not only in the romances that patience is seen to be related in an essential way to redeeming power. Indeed, Marina's restoration of Pericles recalls Cordelia's 'remediate' reunion with Lear, and recalls, too, the fact that we are preached patience out of Shakespeare's deepest tragic abyss:

LEAR: If thou wilt weep my fortunes, take my eyes;
 I know thee well enough; thy name is Gloucester;
 Thou must be patient; we came crying hither:
 Thou know'st the first time that we smell the air
 We wawl and cry. I will preach to thee! mark. (IV. 6)

Gloucester, whose recurring impulse is to succumb to the negations of the tragic experience, never like Lear to explore and be transformed by them, receives this sermon again from his son Edgar:

GLOUCESTER: No farther, sir; a man may rot even here.
EDGAR: What! in ill thoughts again? Men must endure
 Their going hence, even as their coming hither:
 Ripeness is all. Come on.
GLOUCESTER: And that's true too. (IV. 2)

Shakespeare's late romances address themselves to the movement of restoration in Shakespearean tragedy. There is, in these romances, a relaxation of probabilities in order that the possibilities of recovery may be explored, and that the question – what in nature justifies the patience which Lear and Edgar preach? – may be faced. The answer to this question is augured in the exchange between Edgar and Gloucester (indeed, in the *fact* of this exchange; for unknown to Gloucester, Edgar is his son, who will disclose himself later, and, moreover, will become king).

Edgar's remarks look towards the existence of a ripening movement which penetrates even the depths of the tragic abyss. There is a perspective which recognizes that the very possibility of fruition is predicated on a counter-reality of rotting.* This perspective is not only dialectical, in its grasp of the interdependence of these two movements, but transcendental, in the sense of being self-transcending:

'What?! in ill *thoughts* again?' asks Edgar. It is Gloucester's *attitude* that confines him to a darkness which no light penetrates. His despair is a despair which is blind to all possibilities except rotting, and thus is cut off from self-regenerative inspiration. He is,

> Past hope, and in despair; that way, past grace.
> (*Cymbeline*)

But ripeness is all. 'And that's true too.' There are multiple truths, and it is this very multiplicity of truth that opens the way towards a transcendence of individual darks.

A transcendental perspective is, in this sense, included in the very form of *The Winter's Tale*, which moves through three swift and unrelieved acts of tragedy to emerge into the warm light of a pastoral world, peopled by shepherds and clowns. The double potential of life as material for tragedy and comedy is thus realized in a dramatic way. Antigonus brings the child, Perdita, to a desolate shore, which is also the shore of a new world, a world uncorrupted by the tragic passions, a world of comedy and the flow of natural life.

The first inkling of this newness is provided by the clown, a 'natural', who witnesses the destruction of Antigonus' ship by the storm, and of Antigonus himself, by a bear. The natural

* '. . . from hour to hour, we ripe and ripe | And then, from hour to hour, we rot and rot, | And thereby hangs a tale.' – *As You Like It*, II. 7. There can be little doubt that Shakespeare was working consciously in the tradition of the Happy Fall. Cf. *Cymbeline*, v. 4. 94 et seq.

does not see the tragic meaning of what is happening, but only the great destructive motions; he sees suffering, but even suffering has only a secondary place in his vision:

> CLOWN: I would you did but see how it chafes, how it rages, how it takes up the shore! . . . O, the most piteous cry of the poor souls! Sometimes to see 'em, and not to see 'em: now the ship boring the moon with her mainmast, and anon swallowed with yest and froth, as you'd thrust a cork into a hogs-head. And then for the land-service, to see how the bear tore out his shoulder-bone, how he cried to me for help and said his name was Antigonus, a nobleman. But to make an end of the ship, to see how the sea flap-dragoned it: but first how the poor souls roared, and the sea mocked them: and how the poor gentleman roared, and the bear mocked him, both roaring louder than the sea or weather.
>
> (III. 3)

Thus, after making our way to the deepest point of the tragic night, we are made to see from a point of view other than the point of view of tragedy. 'Suddenly, in an outrageous way, the moment we have found most terrible, is seen as if it meant nothing – [we are in] a new world' (Chiappe):

> SHEPHERD: Heavy matters! heavy matters! But look thee here, boy. Now bless thyself: thou met'st with things dying, I with things new born. . . .

The natural wit of the clown is joined by the natural compassion of the shepherd, who has found Perdita, to stay the tragic development. There are perspectives and sympathies in nature which are restorative and healing. The very scope of nature is wider than tragedy; it includes antithetic forces of creation and destruction, antithetic movements of birth and decay. Shakespeare's literary metaphor for this ambiguous and transmutable, and above all expansive world is the final form of his art, a tragical-comical-historical-pastoral mode: romance. His natural image is the sea. The sea is seen even in a single play, such as *Timon*, to have multiple meanings; it is both a salt flood, sterile and destructive, an ultimate image of annihilation, and 'a weeping something, connected to forgiveness' (Chiappe).* The sea entombs and delivers; it is a sea of fortunes carrying men towards both good and evil.

The final sense we are given of the large natural context of these worlds is of a double process, a 'mindless flow' by which life is created and destroyed, an old world passes, a new world is born. There is an attempt in these last plays to see whether man can attune himself to this creative flow and whether he can restore the natural harmonies that the tragic tempest has destroyed. As we have begun to see, a shift in perspective may be a precondition for such regeneration. It may be a precondition as in the enlargement of perspective which involves 'repentance towards reconciliation',† and it may be a precondition as in the enlargement of perspective which surpasses itself towards other truths and towards the possibilities of patience and hope. There is, however, a flow in nature itself which revolutionizes perspectives, and brings new possibilities to birth: the flow of *time*.

In *The Winter's Tale*, the figure of Time (who unfolds all, 'both joy and terror') is introduced as chorus to announce the passage of sixteen years, the emergence of a new generation and the lost child Perdita,

> now grown in grace
> Equal with wond'ring.   (IV. 1)

A new generation brings in its own person new perspectives to life, a wonder, a freshness of compassion and desire, that more weathered generations cannot have. Innocent and ignorant of past guilts and faults, it is able to act as the agent of reconciliation and reunion, to re-tune the harmonies that the older generation in its passion has discordantly and disastrously un-tuned.

---

* ALCIBIADES: . . . rich conceit
    Taught thee to make vast Neptune weep for aye
    On thy low grave, on faults forgiven.   (V. 4)
† 'If a man learns to be able to say that he has been in error, that he has been guilty, he can come to a new sense of things and himself – there can be a recreation of self, paralleling recreation in nature' (Chiappe).

In many ways, the most clearly realized symbol of the regenerative powers of this new generation is Prospero's daughter Miranda. It is she who embodies nature's capacity to produce a wonder, something new, un-ruined by the tragic passions, someone who smiles extremity out of act, who justifies Prosper's patience and hope, the stuff of his endurance within the tragic tempest. She is the wonder who 'quickens what's dead', and inspires in Ferdinand ennobling desire, a desire which finds its life in service, its issue in union, and its fruit in reconciliation, the healing of old wounds and the making of new harmonies.

Miranda not only *is* the wonder, but her capacity for wonder, springing from her youth, is her own special power, her *virtù*. For wonder wakes in her 'the very virtue of compassion', a virtue which is connected to human potential.

> MIRANDA: If by your Art, my dearest father, you have
> Put the wild waters in this roar, allay them . . .
> . . . O, I have suffered
> With those that I saw suffer! a brave vessel,
> (Who had, no doubt, some noble creature in her)
> Dash'd all to pieces. . . .   (I. 2)

Over and over again in this play we are made to witness this wonderful compassion, this instinct towards limitless human possibilities which, at the same time, is often dangerously innocent and naïve, and yet is always necessary if there is to be any room for renewal and rebirth. When Miranda, whose experience of human beings has been limited to Prospero and Ferdinand, is suddenly confronted with a shipload of souls ranging from the evil Antonio through the ambiguous Alonso to the good Gonzalo, she says:

> MIRANDA: O, wonder!
> How many goodly creatures are there here!
> How beauteous mankind is! O brave new world,
> That has such people in 't!   (v. 1)

To which Prospero responds:

> PROSPERO: 'Tis new to thee.

The moment is deftly and wittily poised (the very style of this play is to maintain a self-regarding dimension). Wonder which springs from innocent life is fecund, but not enough to manage, alone, the art of creation. Nature must be nurtured. Even as Miranda's compassion controls Prosper's power, so his power shapes her grace.

Miranda's wonder here has echoes of an earlier witty moment, where the theme of control is more explicitly entered upon. Ferdinand, coming upon Miranda for the first time, takes her to be a goddess and asks if she will remain on the island and how he may 'bear' himself here. Finally he utters his 'prime request, which . . . is',

FERDINAND: . . . O you wonder!
If you be maid or no?   (I. 2)

To which she sweetly replies

MIRANDA: No wonder, sir;
But certainly a maid.

Here the ambiguity between 'I am no wonder' and 'There is no wonder, I am *certainly* a maid' is precious. The chastity of Miranda and Ferdinand (who is made to labour for his love 'lest too light winning make the prize light') is an elaborately and wittily worked-out symbolic theme here, and its wittiness is an important and often overlooked indication of its intention as a direction, not a puritanical code. Here and elsewhere in Shakespeare chastity is sanctioned as a force not to inhibit desire, but to shape it (Chiappe). *

It is the shaping imagination, art, which produces harmonies, music, grace and nobility, human civilization itself. It is art, but an art which nature makes, an imagined order, but an order with real consonances in the world; it is no figment, but founded on deep natural bonds.

Mark how one string, sweet husband to another,
Strikes each in each by mutual ordering,

* In *Pericles*, for example, the Diana who is the play's deity is the three-breasted Diana of the Ephesians, associated with fertility as well as chastity.

> Resembling sire and child and happy mother,
> Who, all in one, one pleasing note do sing --
> (Sonnet 8)

This consonance makes its own lesson. 'The man that hath no music in himself, nor is not mov'd with concord of sweet sounds is fit for treasons, stratagems and spoils'; he is not tuned to the possibilities of order: that an airy nothing can become a harmonious something, that a brutish animal shout can subdue itself into a lyrical human song. Life tuned to concord can be a music, something lovely, and fertile in its own loveliness.

Endurance, then, is justified by the fact of renewal, the force of renewal in man and nature: bonds and orders, harmonies that can come into being, and new compassionate life that can tune them. In part, endurance is made possible by the stoic recognition of ripeness and its connection with rotting, a knowledge that what is not lost cannot be found, an aesthetic recognition that life is a 'defect perfection', its perfection seen as in some essential way lodged in its defect; for the ground of every spring is a winter, of every birth, a death.

In part, endurance is justified by a recognition that is not stoic at all, namely: recognition of the possibilities of transformation. One metaphor for these possibilities, embodying the central theme of perception, is contained in Lear's plea uttered from the sulphurous pit of his tragic vision:

> Give me an ounce of civet, good apothecary,
> To sweeten my imagination. (IV. 6)

Civet is perfume, but it is made from animal flux, dung.* Thus, in an ironic (and here, even bitter) way, Lear touches the core truth of the ideal of civilization: the transubstantiation of nature's dungy presence into a perfumed world.

---

* At least for Shakespeare: 'Civet is of a baser birth than tar, the very uncleanly flux of a cat' (*As You Like It*, III. 2).

There is, finally, the recognition that

> We are such stuff
> As dreams are made on . . .   (IV. I)

not merely dreams as illusions, but dreams as possibilities (like Cleopatra's dream of an emperor Antony) which could be made into the real. Life is the ground of such visions, of pageants which are necessarily insubstantial and musics which are airy nothings. Unbridled passions, unchecked self-interests can dissolve the revel (as in *The Tempest* they do), can kill the potential of life's feast. To preserve this potential and to resurrect it, requires a compassion, a fertile grace.

Imagination is a way to the fullness of experience, and to its harmony and order. And because it is a way to order, to a design and epic of being beyond mere contingency and presence, imagination shares in creation. For man is a creation of the orders in which he participates, the orders that raise his creatureliness to humanity and set the stage on which his nobility can be enacted.

TWO

The Bonds of Human Kindness

The Bonds of Human Kindness

I. FACT AND VALUE

For Shakespeare, as for the Renaissance, order is *constitutive*, and not merely a regulative concept. Creatures and things are conceived as participating in particular orders of being. In this view, man, by virtue of his free-will, has the possibility of ascending or descending a Great Chain of Being, in accordance with the pattern of his own existence, whether reason rules his senses, or whether gross sensuality has sway over his reason. ('I choose myself not in my being, but in my manner of being' – Sartre.)

Social order is also constitutive. For Shakespeare, the collapse of social and familial bonds means the collapse of generic human forms, leaving force as the determinant of basic order. When force has become ultimate arbiter, right and wrong 'lose their names' and 'everything includes itself in power'. Then power is included into will, will into appetite,

> And appetite, a universal wolf,
> So doubly seconded with will and power
> Must make perforce a universal prey,
> And last eat up himself.
>
> (*Troilus and Cressida*, I. 3)

The disruption of civil and familial bonds is seen as releasing a wolfish appetite, and this appetite, reinforced by human will and human power, begets a 'chaos' as empty of human reality and as sterile of human purpose as the primal chaos, itself, before creation.

In other words, the fabric of human order and of human existence is one fabric, knit by bonds whose ontological function makes them assume the role of human *values*. The destruction of the values means the destruction of both the order and its reality. This existential view is a decisive break with the Tudor concept that man's *actual* social reality expresses a divine order, and that violation of this order, rebellion against the *status quo*, will bring down divine retribution on the transgressor.

Over and over in Shakespeare, and with an insistence in the late plays that makes it impossible to ignore, rebellion against feudal or socially sanctioned allegiance is expressly demanded in the name of a *human* order. In *Cymbeline*, for example, when Posthumus' servant Pisanio disobeys his master's command to murder Imogen, and thus breaks his social bond, he justifies his action in the following significant terms:

> PISANIO: How? that I should murder her,
>   Upon the love and truth and vows which I
>   Have made to thy command? I, her? Her blood?
>   If it be so to do good service, never
>   Let me be counted serviceable. *How look I,*
>   *That I should seem to lack humanity*
>   *So much as this fact* [crime] *comes to?*   (III. 2)

Pisanio's refusal to violate his own humanity is no minor incident in the play's action, moreover. It is the central mechanism averting the tragedy towards which events have been headed, and prepares the ground for the innocent Imogen's phoenix-like 'resurrection'. Nor is his act of isolated significance, for both Camillo, in *The Winter's Tale*, and Gonzalo, in *The Tempest*, perform parallel and equally central roles. They disregard or countermand their socially sanctioned vows when these vows violate their human conscience, and by their acts they arrest the tragic courses, and prepare the way for the 'redemptions' which follow.

These romances, of course, are statements of the great Shakespearean positives, their 'simplicities' those distillations characteristic of the late works of many major artists. To bring the structure of a Shakespearean ethic into multidimensional perspective, therefore, it is necessary to approach also from the side of complexity, which means, in this case, to turn back to the 'dark period' that precedes the great tragedies and lodges one of the most disconcerting visions in the Shakespearean spectrum: *Troilus and Cressida*.

The play *Troilus and Cressida*, classified in the Quarto edition of 1609 as a comedy and in the Folio as a tragedy, presents us with a world in which there is an unbridgeable gap between fact and value, between actual human behaviour and the principles that men take to be binding upon their actions. The play is set in the Trojan War, whose related episodes and myths functioned in the Greek canon as a kind of Genesis, not least because they engage, as themes, the central values that bind men's private and public lives. These themes are love and honour: the one redeems the lust for bodies, which man shares with beasts, into something richer and more lasting, and thus 'humanizes' man's intimate relations; the other transforms his lust for power into service, and thus channels his brutish energies into avenues of noble action.

The rift at the centre of all human action, in the world of Shakespeare's play, can be read immediately in the figure of Helen, who, as the subject of the war, is at once the centre of the world and the symbol of its disintegration.

> PARIS: . . . tell me noble Diomed, faith, tell me true,
>   Even in the soul of sound good-fellowship
>   Who in your thoughts, deserves fair Helen best,
>   Myself or Menelaus?   (IV. I)

The language of Paris' question ('noble', 'faith', 'true') is the language of the ghost order of value that haunts this world and conflicts so violently with its reality. Diomed's reply dissolves the mists of Paris' rhetoric and translates its significances into their proper terms. Both Paris and Menelaus, answers Diomed, deserve Helen alike for,

> DIOMED: [Menelaus] like a puling cuckold, would drink up
>   The lees and dregs of a flat tamed piece.

You, like a lecher, out of whorish loins
Are pleased to breed out your inheritors. . . .

The sordidness of Paris' and Menelaus' quarrel is no private
squalor, however; it is the squalor of human destiny itself, in this
world, polluting human purposes and poisoning human lives:

DIOMED: Hear me, Paris.
For every false drop in her bawdy veins
A Grecian's life hath sunk; for every scruple
Of her contaminated carrion weight
A Trojan hath been slain. Since she could speak,
She hath not given so many good words breath
As for her Greeks and Trojans suffered death.

A contaminated carrion weight dominates this world, binding to
its diseased core the sinews of all human enterprise. Moreover,
Diomed himself is incorporated into this corruption, for it defines
all social endeavour. A prince of the Grecian army, Diomed's
social being is defined by his role in furthering the Greek cause,
which is to repossess this Helen. It involves him in a hypocrisy, at
this point, which Paris does not fail to mark:

PARIS: Fair Diomed, you do as chapmen do
Dispraise the thing that you desire to buy –

Appetite drives the world; it is the motive force of its central
public action. In such a context, where honour and reason suc-
ceed in being socially operative, they necessarily become agents of
the very forces they are intended to keep in check. Thus when
the possibility of returning Helen to her husband is raised in the
Trojan camp, the issue has really been decided beforehand and
Trojan 'honour' merely reinforces this decision.

'Pleasure and revenge', as Hector says in the debate, 'have ears
more deaf than adders to the voice of any true decision.' Revenge is
the Greek motive in the war, pleasure – (the theft of Helen) –
essentially, the Trojan. It is Troilus, who makes clear that these
primary motives and their attendant decisions have pre-decided
all secondary questions. When Paris 'brought home the noble

prize', he recalls, the Trojans 'all clapped hands and cried "Inestimable" '. 'What's aught,' argues Troilus, 'but as 'tis valued?' Once the Trojans have made a choice, their honour is at stake in adhering to it, and the value of their honour, being absolute for them, must be decisive. The Trojans cannot return today what they coveted yesterday without admitting 'that we have stol'n what we do fear to keep!', that their original action was base and that they are cowards as well. On the other hand, they can preserve the integrity of their honour, and 'prove' the 'value' of Helen, in Troilus' view, by continuing to hold her against the Grecian armies.

This argument convinces Hector not of its rightness (for, as he says, ''Tis mad idolatry to make the service greater than the god'), but of its necessity. Helen must be kept, he agrees, 'For 'tis a cause that hath no mean dependence upon our joint and several dignities.' In other words, no matter what the moral law,[*] or how many lives are thrown away, it is necessary that the Trojans' original desire for Helen be 'justified' by force of arms in order to preserve Trojan 'honour'. Hector's words, says Troilus triumphantly, touch the 'life' of the Trojan design, which is not lust but 'glory' (i.e. pride). Helen is

> ... a theme of honour and renown,
> A spur to valiant and magnanimous deeds
> Whose present courage may beat down our foes,
> And fame in time to come canonize us. (II. 2)

The word 'canonize' unmasks the pretence, however unconscious, with which language is being used here, and reveals the essential mystification of meanings in this world. For to proclaim the possibility of seizing sanctification through fame by force of arms, as Troilus does, is to project on to power the one possibility that it does not have; it is to affirm the doctrine of might makes right and thus to invert the whole design of cosmic order, to turn what is absolute into the merely contingent and what is contingent into the absolute. Indeed, in a world in which appetite functions as

---

[*] 'Moral laws of nature and of nations speak aloud to have her back returned' – Hector.

primary value, it is the fate of all religious and moral codes that do not reject the 'world' and its worldly values outright, to be fetishistic, to elevate things to the status of absolutes, to turn whores like Helen into gods, and to bind objects of self-seeking desire into a structure of sanctifying values.

With the acceptance of a system in which self-interest is the basis of order, honour becomes merely a context for winning self-glory, morality a phantom structure allowing those 'fools of Time' to '. . . die for goodness, who have liv'd for crime'.* Those warriors, like Hector, whose absolute is but a 'child of state' shore up false values with their valour while Fortune smiles on them, but when she frowns, are caught up by their very commitment in the mesh gears of Machiavellian intrigue and unprincipled action. Thus socially sanctioned honour merely strengthens the Machiavellian basis of a corrupt social order; once engaged in such a world, honour must hold to the dictum that whatever is, is right.

Just as the ideal of honour, as distinct from its practice, aims at transcending mere appetite and self-interest in the public sphere, so the ideal of love is a principle of transcendence in the private sphere. The fate of the two ideals in the disintegrated world context of *Troilus and Cressida* is in fact parallel, marked by their divorce first from 'reality' and then from their own meanings.

As appetite rules in the public sphere of politics in *Troilus and Cressida*, so it dominates the sphere of love. Paris, whose 'love' has caused the war, and who thus is a reminder of the interdependence of the spheres, defines love for Helen and Pandar. 'Hot blood', says Paris, 'begets hot thoughts, and hot thoughts beget hot deeds, and hot deeds is love.'

A counter-view to Paris' cynicism is held by Troilus, who is cast as a chivalric figure, a prince of courtly lovers. In a world so given over to sensuality, however, the only romance one would expect to survive would be a romance embodying flight from reality. Such, indeed, is Troilus' romance. As he waits in the orchard to meet Cressida and to consummate his love, Troilus' sense is 'enchanted' by 'the imaginary relish' and his chief fear is that the

* Sonnet 124.

reality to come cannot possibly equal this expectant moment. His 'ruder' senses (that is his non-imagining senses), he fears, have not the capacity to receive the experience. It will be 'some joy too fine, too subtle-potent, tun'd too sharp in sweetness' to be sensed.

Not only a flight from the deed of love is embodied in Troilus' romanticism, but a flight from the object of his love as well. Thus it is his lot to dote on a consummate sensualist ('her wanton spirits look out at every joint and motive of her body' – Ulysses) and believe, of necessity, that she is a blushing virgin.

The contrast between the outlooks of Troilus and Cressida is brought into sharp relief when they confront one another. Perceiving that Troilus loves by the book, Cressida, in Machiavellian fashion, shapes her image to his passion and lets him believe that she is frightened by the prospect of 'hot deeds'. Troilus reassures her:

TROILUS: Oh, let my lady apprehend no fear. In all Cupid's pageant there is presented no monster.

CRESSIDA: Nor nothing monstrous neither?

TROILUS: Nothing but our undertakings – when we vow to weep seas, live in fire, eat rocks, tame tigers, thinking it harder for our mistress to devise imposition enough than for us to undergo any difficulty imposed. This is the monstruosity in love, lady, that the will is infinite and the execution confined, that the desire is boundless and the act a slave to limit.

(III. 2)

What Troilus is referring to is the heroic service of the lady which chivalric lovers perform. He is ruefully aware of the degree to which both the literary image and his own aspiration outstrip the possibilities of reality. He can find no performable metaphor equal to the size of his love. In other words, the subject of his discourse is chivalric service, that sublimation of energies which transforms the final gift of love into grace. Cressida's mind, however, proves incapable of rising to this conception and in one of the most piquant misconstruings in literature, she replies:

CRESSIDA: They say all lovers swear more performance than they are able, and yet reserve an ability that they never

perform, vowing more than the perfection of ten, and dis-
charging less than the tenth part of one. They that have the
voice of lions and the act of hares, are they not monsters?

Thus the monsters in Cupid's pageant for Cressida, are those men
who boast of a sexual prowess which, on actual testing, they do
not have. As for Troilus' truth, his service of faith, it means nothing
to her, for whom romance is but a dressing for the deed.

The chasm between these lovers' worlds is impossibly wide and,
in the end, results in crisis. When Cressid's betrayal finally becomes visible to Troilus, it provokes a split between his troth and
his truth, between his faith and his cognition, between his values
and his reality, which parallels the split in the larger realm. His
resolution of the split, moreover, takes a similar course.

Like Hector, Troilus lacks the duplicity that characterizes the
norm of behaviour in the world. The moral of his wit is 'plain and
true'; there is integrity between his word and his deed. It is just
this integrity that throws him into crisis when he beholds Cressid
in the act of betrayal: 'This is, and is not, Cressid', he cries. The
image and being of his love, the ideal and reality both lodged in
Cressida (as in the world they are lodged in Helen), a thing seem-
ingly indivisible, in the act of betrayal 'divides more wider than
the sky and earth', and yet it reveals no opening, no space of
division: 'this is, and is not, Cressid'.

To resolve this contradiction in the structure of reality is not
possible without rejecting this 'world' itself. For the structure of
reality of this world is essentially valueless, it is knit not with the
'eternal' bonds of heaven, but with bonds of short-term self-
interest. To treat such bonds as absolutes, as Troilus and Hector
do, is to invite disillusion and destruction. To operate within the
atomistic assumptions of such a framework, as the other chief in-
habitants of this world (including Ulysses) do, is to resolve everything into power and appetite and thus to invite the chaos that
chokes all *human* enterprise.

Troilus fails, however, to face the crisis that confronts him in its
real implications. For while he accepts the fact of Cressida's false-

ness, it does not lead him to question the basis and meaning of his faith. He remains true to the whole course of illusion-filled action that has brought him to the crisis, and to the code of values that has failed him in the actual world. Thus the perfidy of Cressida does not signal the collapse of his faith, nor does it impel him to destroy or abandon the corrupted centre of his love, to yield her up as the Trojans should have yielded up Helen. Rather, he is governed by his earlier position that honour must stand by its commitments however corrupt they prove in practice. He resolves to preserve his honour and the meaning of his 'fancy'* by revenging himself on Diomed, who is merely the receiver of Cressida's cheaply held bounty:

TROILUS: Much as I do Cressid love,
   So much by weight hate I her Diomed; . . .   (v. 2)

In resolving to make war on Diomed, in essence to preserve his honour, Troilus recapitulates in his own story the story of the war itself: a cuckold, deserted by a faithless wife, lays siege against the lecher who has 'stolen' her. A war with such a basis cannot be anything other than a universal competition to earn honours and gain glories that are corrupted in their very core. Achilles' foul murder of the unarmed Hector emphasizes the inescapable truth: there can be no honour, no authentic value, within an enterprise, a structure of enterprises, where value is divorced from fact, where socially effective 'interest' is not an interest in truth, or trust, or human ends, but in self, in the dictates of self-will, appetite, and power.

II. COMMODITY AND CHAOS

The total impasse reached in *Troilus and Cressida*, which is a play without a resolution, and reflected in Troilus' nihilistic outburst at the end ('linger not our sure destructions . . .') is rare in

---

* 'Fancy' is Troilus' word and the proper one. 'Never', he says, 'did young man fancy with so eternal and fixed a soul.' And this is precisely the point. He fancies as other men love, i.e. absolutely. He converts an object of desire into an object of faith. This is idolatory, fetishism of an extreme kind.

Shakespeare and deserves the closest attention. For in drawing its conflicts to unresolvable extremes, the play has made visible aspects of Shakespeare's conception of a world structure that otherwise might have remained obscure.

Another way of viewing the central opposition in the play is to see it as a tension between order and disorder, or rather a tension between an outlived order, which is external to and stands above self-seeking appetite, and an actual disorder, which is the product of a world dominated by anarchic individual desires. The thematic importance to Shakespearean tragedy of the tension between self-interested evil and the compassionate recognition of natural bonds has long been noted. What has generally been ignored by students of Shakespeare, however, is the central place occupied by this conflict in the social life and thought of Shakespeare's time:

> The England of the Reformation, to which posterity turns as a source of high debates on church government and doctrine, was to contemporaries a cauldron seething with economic unrest and social passions. . . . In England, as on the Continent, the new economic realities came into sharp collision with the social theory inherited from the Middle Ages. . . .*

How seriously Shakespeare considered this collision and its reverberations can be gleaned from one of his relatively early histories, *King John*. The question of central surface concern in this play is the source of right in society. To pose the question, Shakespeare chose a normally unstressed aspect of John's reign, namely, the problem of his nephew Arthur's claim to the throne. For in feudal society, the effective source of right is the king,

---

* '. . . There is no place in medieval theory for economic activity which is not related to a moral end, and to found a science of society upon the assumption that appetite for economic gain is a . . . force, to be accepted, like other natural forces, . . . would have appeared to the medieval thinker as hardly less irrational or less immoral than to make the premise of social philosophy the unrestrained operation of such necessary human attributes as pugnacity or the sexual instinct. . . . Riches, as St Antonio says, exist for man, not man for riches . . .' – R. H. Tawney, *Religion and the Rise of Capitalism*, London, John Murray, 1927.

who is in theory the deputy of heaven. In theory, the king is *naturally* endowed, that is by blood, with the moral attributes befitting his role, as well as with the hereditary prerogatives of kingly power.

John's hereditary right to the throne and its power is challenged by Arthur, seconded by King Philip of France; but John is confident that he will retain it:

KING JOHN: Our strong possession and our right for us. (I. 1)

To which his mother, Queen Elinor, rejoins:

ELINOR: Your strong possession much more than your right.

We are thus made at once aware that power and right are at odds in this world, an awareness that is deliberately and ingeniously intensified as the action develops:

ELINOR: I can produce
  A will that bars the title of thy son.
CONSTANCE: Ay, who doubts that? a will! a wicked will;
  A woman's will, a cank'red grandam's will!   (II. 1)

where the single word 'will', as both a binding legal form and self-serving desire, embodies the main meaning.

When the opposing armies of England confront one another before the English-controlled town of Angiers, the two claimants call upon the town's citizens to recognize their respective titles to the throne. But the citizens of Angiers cannot recognize the true kingly presence, and we are reminded, momentarily, of Aeneas' cynical remarks in *Troilus and Cressida* when he enters the Greek camp and seeks Agamemnon.

AENEAS: How may
  A stranger to those most imperial looks
  Know them from eyes of other mortals?   (I. 3)

To this query Angiers finds an answer. The true king will prove himself by defeating the false king: might will make right.

The claimants, who have understood all along that the integrity of blood will be 'proved' by the spilling of blood, fight, but without either side winning victory. The impasse which results is solved by a political marriage which buys the King of France from his allegiance to Arthur.

The commentary on this perjury at the centre of the world is appropriately made by the 'illegitimate' Faulconbridge. It offers penetrating insight into Shakespeare's vision of the roots of social disorder:*

> Mad world! mad kings! mad composition!
> John, to stop Arthur's title in the whole,
> Hath willingly departed with a part:
> And France, whose armour *conscience* buckled on,
> Whom *zeal* and *charity* brought to the field
> As *God's own soldier*, rounded in the ear
> With that same *purpose-changer*, that *sly divel*,
> That *broker*, that still *breaks the pate of faith*,
> That daily *break-vow*, he that wins of all,
> Of kings, of beggars, old men, young men, maids, . . .
> That smooth-fac'd gentleman, tickling *commodity*,
> *Commodity*, the bias of the world, . . .
> Hath drawn [France] from his own determin'd aid,
> From a resolv'd and honourable war,
> To a most base and vile-concluded peace.

Commodity is the bias of the world, 'bias' being the lead weight on one side of bowls which causes them to swerve from a direct course. Hence commodity is the bias that makes the world swerve from its true path.

The word 'commodity' had somewhat different implications for the Elizabethans from those it has now. From its root sense, 'convenience', it derived such meanings as 'expediency', 'benefit', 'advantage', 'profit', 'interest: often in the sense of profit or selfish interest, gain'. It was associated with trading and particularly with

---

* And thus provides an important complement to Ulysses' famous speech on degree: 'The heavens themselves, the planets and this centre, | Observe degree, priority and place, | Insisture, course, proportion, season . . .' (I. 3)

usurious interest, a fact that intensified its derogative overtones. For moral resistance to the new capitalist order in the sixteenth century centred on the resistance to usury, which meant then not only money-lending, but any attempt to profit in a bargain at the expense of the other party, to achieve advantage for oneself by exploiting another person's weakness or need.*

The principle of commodity, as self-interested gain or profit, standing above all other values and becoming, in fact, the prime mover, the lord of the world, is precisely the Bastard's meaning:

> Since kings break faith upon commodity,
> Gain, be my lord, for I will worship thee.

'The world . . . of itself', according to the Bastard, 'is peised well' (balanced), and 'made to run on even ground'. Order, the same order of which Ulysses speaks, is a *natural* order, the order of all creation. It is commodity that unbalances this order, that untunes this harmonious structure, upsets this creative form, and leads the world into disordered, discordant, and destructive chaos. For it is commodity, this 'advantage, this vile-drawing bias, this sway of motion', that makes the world 'take head from [i.e. rush away from] all indifferency [equity, absence of bias], from all direction, purpose, course, intent'. It is commodity that destroys faith, upsets law, breaks the bonds of love and honour, commodity

> This bawd, this broker,† this all-changing word.‡

* 'Not only the taking of interest for a loan, but the raising of prices by a monopolist, the beating down of prices by a keen bargainer, the rack-renting of land by a landlord, the sub-letting of land by a tenant at a rent higher than he himself paid, the cutting of wages . . . the excessive profits of a middle-man – all these were among the "unlawful chaffer", the "subtlety and sleight", which was what the plain man who sat on juries and listened to sermons in parish churches meant by usury [in the sixteenth century].' – Tawney.

† 'Broker: a retailer of commodities, a second-hand dealer, a pawn-broker, a money-lender, a middleman, a go-between in love affairs, a match-maker, a procurer, pimp, bawd; a pander generally' – e.g. 'Hence broker, lackie!' (Troilus to Pandar).

‡ 'All-changing word' is a pun on commodity's double role as a principle of commercial exchange and a changer of faith, of values.

Shakespeare reiterates this important view in his most bitter play, *Timon of Athens*. Digging for roots (in a double sense, for sustenance and the source of renewal), Timon finds gold instead, the 'fair angel' (a gold coin) of commodity in the Bastard's scheme:

> Earth, yield me roots.
> . . . What is here?
> Gold? Yellow, glittering, precious gold?
> . . . Thus much of this will make
> Black, white; foul, fair; wrong, right;
> Base, noble; old, young; coward, valiant. . . .
> This yellow slave
> Will knit and break religions, bless th'accurs'd. . . .
>
> (IV. 3)

Gold as (unnatural) coinage dissolves all distinctions, destroys all order, purpose, faith;* it is the antithesis of natural roots, and its destructive effect on natural creative order makes sense of Timon's apparently misanthropic outburst:

> Earth, yield me roots.
> Who seeks for better of thee, sauce his palate
> With thy most operant poison. . . .

Timon is, of course, Shakespeare's most negative vision and unique in that respect. Elsewhere in the plays, there is an active confrontation of orders, a struggle between commodity and the bonds it negates, which forms the centre of Shakespeare's concern. In order to explore this centre, the sense of certain concepts that underwent decisive transformation as a result of the social transformations of the sixteenth and seventeenth centuries must first be recaptured.

---

* Cf. Marx's commentary on this passage in the *Economic and Philosophical Manuscripts*: 'If *money* is the bond binding me to *human* life, binding society to me, binding me and nature and man, is not money the bond of all *bonds*? Can it not dissolve and bind all ties? Is it not, therefore, the universal *agent of divorce*? . . .'

The law of nature had been invoked by medieval writers as a moral restraint upon economic self-interest.* By the seventeenth century a significant revolution had taken place. 'Nature' had come to connote, not divine-ordinance, but human appetites, and natural rights were invoked by the individualism of the age as a reason why self-interest should be given free play. . . . (Tawney)

When Antonio, in *The Merchant of Venice*, suggests that it is wrong to take back more money than one originally loans, Shylock defends the practice of charging interest as recompense for thrift. In support of the practice, he recalls the Biblical story of Jacob and Laban who shared a herd of sheep. By skilful breeding, Jacob produced more parti-coloured lambs than others in the herd, and these, as had been agreed beforehand, then belonged to him; adds Shylock,

> This was a way to thrive, and he was blest:
> And thrift is blessing if men steal it not. (I. 3)

To this Antonio replies that the production of lambs was not in Jacob's power to bring to pass, but was 'fashion'd by the hand of heaven'. The story, he concludes, does not justify interest,

> . . . Or is your gold and silver ewes and rams?

To which Shylock answers,

> I cannot tell, I make it breed as fast, – . . .

Shylock conceives himself to be a breeder of money, and thus places his profession firmly in Nature's (new) order.

---

* '. . . the usurer is most rightly hated, because money itself is the source of his gain, and is not used for the purposes for which it was invented. For it originated for the exchange of commodities, but interest makes out of money, more money . . . so that of all modes of making a living, this is the most contrary to Nature.' – Aristotle, *Politics*.

This minor moment shows how Shakespeare's ear was sensitive to this social issue. Indeed, the central artifice in *The Merchant of Venice*, the bond between Shylock and Antonio, is constructed in such a way as to express the conflict at the heart of the transformation of social values in the period.

When Antonio asks Shylock for a loan, he does so not because he needs the money for business purposes or for his own gain, but for his friend Bassanio, who has come to him for help. When Antonio asks Shylock for money, however, he does so not as one friend to another. On the contrary, he hardly considers Shylock a fellow human being, a fact which Shylock himself stresses. Yet Antonio seeks from Shylock what one can seek only from a fellow human being, namely help. A human being can give help, however, only if he is governed not by appetite and self-interest, but by generosity and kindness.

Thus, when Antonio asks Shylock whether he shall be beholden to him (and there is an ambiguity in the word 'beholden' which can mean indebted either morally or contractually), the usurer takes the opportunity to stress the paradoxical nature of their bond:

> SHYLOCK: Well then, it now appears you need my help:
> Go to then, you come to me, and you say,
> 'Shylock, we would have moneys,' you say so:
> You that did void your rheum upon my beard,
> And foot me as you spurn a stranger cur
> Over your threshold, moneys is your suit.
> What should I say to you? Should I not say
> 'Hath a dog money? is it possible
> A cur can lend three thousand ducats?' or . . .
> 'Fair sir, you spet on me on Wednesday last,
> You call'd me dog: and for these courtesies
> I'll lend you this much moneys'?

The hollowness of the moral obligation which Shylock owes to Antonio, as a fellow human being, is obvious; hence, his 'help' can only be bought.

While Antonio's attitude to Shylock, personally, has been an un-Christian one, he has used Christian principles in trade as a means of inflicting even further injury on Shylock, for he 'lends out money gratis and brings down the rate of usance' particularly among Shylock's clients. It is upon these grounds that Shylock devises his scheme to pay Antonio back, offering to lend the money he desires at no interest (an apparently 'Christian' gesture) but to take a pound of flesh if the bond is forfeit.

> SHYLOCK: I would be friends with you, . . .
> Supply your present wants, and take no doit
> Of usance for my moneys, . . .
> This is kind I offer.
> BASSANIO: This were kindness.
> SHYLOCK: This kindness will I show.

In this exchange, where Shylock introduces his 'bargain', the play on the words 'kind' and 'kindness' is, of course, crucial. It is, as we shall see, also crucial for the larger question at hand.

'Kind' for the Elizabethans and for preceding periods referred first of all to nature. It meant 'native', 'implanted by nature', 'innate', 'naturally fitting', 'belonging to this particular natural kind or species', hence also 'related by kinship', something held 'by right of birth', 'lawful', 'rightful', 'kindly'.

By extension, the word applied also to the *quality* of its kind. It meant having the natural qualities developed. Thus: 'The kindest Mastiffe when he is clapped on the back, fighteth best' (1579). The truest to kind, moreover, would naturally tend to be associated with the best of its kind, hence 'kind' also took on the meaning 'of good kind', 'well-born', 'well-bred', of 'gentle [i.e. noble] birth'.

In its Elizabethan form, therefore, the word 'kind' possesses both an ontological and an ethical dimension. It is in its application to persons, moreover, that this two-dimensional aspect of the word takes on its real significance. For 'kind' as applied to persons means 'naturally well disposed; having a gentle, sympathetic, or benevolent nature; ready to assist or show consideration for others; generous, liberal, courteous; bearing good-will, friendly disposition, affection, loving,* thankful, grateful'. In other words, *to be kind (human) is to be kind*: to possess the generic human qualities of love, compassion, generosity, gratefulness, gentleness, benevolence, etc. To be human is to be humane.

The subsequent divorce between the ethical and ontological dimensions of the word 'kind' is clearly related to the transformation in the sense of nature in this epoch, to which Tawney refers.† For if, before the economic revolution of the sixteenth and seventeenth centuries, to be natural was to be kind, by the end of that revolution the emergence of a new socio-economic order had assured the ascendance of a new ideology of nature, which sanctioned as 'natural' the new economic realities and the ethics of self-interest that these 'realities' required; thereby it rendered the very notion of the equivalence of kindness (humaneness) and nature obsolete.

When Shylock, who represents the new order, uses the word 'kind' ('This kindness will I show') his primary meaning is 'nature', in the sense of 'Antonio's kind', and only in a mocking sense 'generous'. This meaning is confirmed when, finally, it becomes apparent that Antonio's bond will be forfeit, and Shylock is asked what benefit he will reap from Antonio's pound of flesh. His answer is: it will be payment *in kind*.

> SALARINO: Why, I am sure if he forfeit thou wilt not take his flesh, – what's that good for?
>
> SHYLOCK: To bait fish withal, – if it will feed nothing else, it will feed my revenge; he hath disgrac'd me, and hind'red me half a million, laugh'd at my losses, mock'd my gains, scorned my nation, . . . If a Jew wrong a Christian, what is his humility? revenge! If a Christian wrong a Jew, what should his sufferance be by Christian example? – why, revenge! *The villiany you teach me I will execute*, and it shall go hard but I will better the instruction.   (III. 1)

---

* 'Women are kind by kind, but coy by fashion' (1594).
† Epigraph, p. 115 above.

In view of Shylock's intent that the bond between them should be a bond of affinity between his own and Antonio's method of dealing with enemies, Antonio's early remark on concluding the agreement acquires a mordant irony:

ANTONIO: Hie thee gentle* Jew
The Hebrew will turn Christian, he grows kind.   (I. 3)

The bond that Antonio seals with Shylock has a larger significance, however, which is revealed only by an examination of the meaning of another germinal word, namely, *bond*. 'Bond' or 'band' in its primary meaning signifies a fetter, a negative restraint. A bondman is a slave or serf, hence Shylock's use:

SHYLOCK: Shall I bend low, and in a bondman's key
With bated breath, and whisp'ring humbleness
Say this:
Fair sir, you spet on me on Wednesday last, . . .

'Bondman' or 'bondsman' applies, however, to other feudal relations besides that of master and serf, as for example bonds of feudal allegiance between nobles and kings. Hence a bond is also an obligation, a duty. At the same time, embedded in these negative senses, there is a positive dimension. This positive dimension shows itself in the phrase 'our lady's bonds' which signifies 'pregnancy', '*confinement* at childbirth', a restraint which makes possible creation. In a similar direction, a bond is also 'a cementing force or influence by which a union of any kind is maintained', as in the 'bonds of matrimony'. The idea of an organic relation, a binding that holds in being a creative union, is central to the Shakespearean conception: the bonds of family, of society, of humanity, of nature, are bonds that band men together and bind them from chaos, and bear them in continual renewal and regeneration.

The difference between these human bonds, whose end is human life, and the commercial bond that Shylock and Antonio seal is rooted in the difference between the old philosophy of

* A pun on 'gentile'.

society and the new. 'Society', in the perspective of the new order, 'is not a community of classes with varying functions, united to each other by mutual obligations arising from a common end. It is a joint-stock company rather than an organism, and the liabilities of the shareholders are strictly limited' (Tawney).

It is precisely this concept of limited human bonds which Shakespeare exposes to devastating ridicule in the courtroom scene, as Shylock prepares to collect the pound of flesh due him, according to the bond:

> PORTIA: Have by some surgeon, Shylock, on your charge,
>   To stop his wounds, lest he do bleed to death.
> SHYLOCK: Is it so nominated in the bond?
> PORTIA: It is not so express'd, but what of that?
>   'Twere good you do so much for charity.
> SHYLOCK: I cannot find it, 'tis not in the bond.   (IV. I)

Human responsibilities and obligations, in Shylock's view, end in the terms of the bond. Moreover, the terms of the bond are dictated by its limited purpose, which is not human life, but the self-interest of the bonded parties. What makes the bond inhuman, therefore, is its inhuman basis and order, the fact that 'commodity' is its primal principle, its lord. The bond is not a bond of essential union, but of essential conflict;* it is a bond in whose terms one human being seeks to gain advantage at the expense of another, to exploit rather than to answer his human need.

Whether explicitly or implicitly, human bonds, which constitute the structure of human life, whose violation is a breach in nature, and upon whose destruction there follows chaos and a sterile choking, are central to Shakespeare's ethical conception. It is for this reason that the bond which knits the plot of *The Merchant of Venice* assumes such overriding significance. For it is not a bond of common humanity expressing some positive human connection but a usurious bond, a 'commodity' bond, in which the exploitation of human dependence is the primary goal. Shylock disclaims

---

* ANTONIO: If thou wilt lend this money, lend it not | As to thy friends; for when did friendship take | A breed for barren metal of his friend?   (I. 3)

any such intention, but in driving home the bargain later reveals the true colour of his hypocrisy.

Initially disclaiming any ulterior motive, Shylock contends that the pound of flesh that he might demand on forfeit of the bond cannot mean gain for him, for a pound of human flesh is practically worthless in a commercial scale of value:

> SHYLOCK: A pound of man's flesh taken from a man,
> Is not so estimable, profitable neither
> As flesh of muttons, beefs, or goats, – . . .   (I. 3)

A 'good man' in Shylock's terms, as he explains earlier, is a 'sufficient' man, i.e. one whose credit is good. But however 'real' Shylock's scale of value is for the new economic order (and one must not underestimate the impact of this 'reality', even then), it is not adequate from a human point of view. Men are not cattle. There are values that transcend market values and in whose terms, ultimately – at least for Shakespeare – the market must justify itself. Thus the pound of flesh, which is a surety for the agreement, also serves to emphasize the bond of flesh, the human bond, which is absent from their commercial contract and, further, to emphasize the human meaning of their contract. For in the end, it is *Antonio*'s pound of flesh and not merely a pound of human meat to which Shylock will have access, and this fact makes it valuable to him, whatever the market price.

There is, thus, a natural bond between Antonio and Shylock. They confront one another as human beings, not merely commercial agents, and it is in this bond that their antagonism festers:

> SHYLOCK: . . . he hath disgrac'd me, . . . heated mine
> enemies, – and what's his reason? I am a Jew. Hath not a
> Jew eyes? hath not a Jew hands, . . .   (III. 1)

When Antonio forfeits the bond, he is put at the mercy of Shylock, who is given absolute power over him. It is, moreover, the *law* of Venice that gives him this unnatural and unjust power, and it does so because it is shaped to commercial, not natural, ends. The fact that the law empowers Shylock to murder Antonio for a financial default is of crucial significance. For this is no isolated occurrence. The commercial law of Venice enforces other un-natural and inhuman ends, as Shylock, who in an ironic way is the conscience of this world, is quick to point out:

> DUKE: How shalt thou hope for mercy rend'ring none?
> SHYLOCK: What judgment shall I dread doing no wrong?
>   You have among you many a purchas'd slave,
>   Which (like your asses, and your dogs and mules)
>   You use in abject and in slavish parts,
>   Because you *bought* them, – shall I say to you,
>   Let them be free, marry them to your heirs?
>   Why sweat they under burthens? let their beds
>   Be made as soft as yours, and let their palates
>   Be season'd with such viands? you will answer
>   'The slaves are ours,' – so do I answer you:
>   The pound of flesh (which I demand of him)
>   Is dearly bought, 'tis mine and I will have it:
>   If you deny me, fie upon your law!
>   There is no force in the decrees of Venice:
>   I stand for judgment, – answer, shall I have it?   (IV. I)

Thus Shylock makes the critical observation to be made about this order. If you buy something, even a human being, you own it, and have the full power of ownership over it. The commercial law of commodity stands above the moral law of kind.

Shylock's contention, furthermore, that the whole fabric of Venetian law is at stake in the enforcement of his inhuman bond is a home-point. Not only Venetian law, but the structure of Venetian wealth, to whose requirements the law has been fashioned, is tied up in Shylock's bond:

> SALARINO: I am sure the duke
>   Will never grant this forfeiture to hold.
> ANTONIO: The duke cannot deny the course of law:
>   For the commodity that strangers have
>   With us in Venice, if it be denied,

Will much impeach the justice of the state,
Since that the trade and profit of the city
Consisteth of all nations. . . .   (III. 3)

In other words, the fact that Venice is a 'world market' means that
the law must be strict in its impartiality and its letter adhered to,
so that foreigners may have faith enough in it to do business
there. For foreigners, who would not know the duke, would be
wary of his judgement in making exceptions to temporize the law,
to keep it in touch with concrete human situations.

Venetian law is not primarily a formal framework expressing
the harmonious and natural order of relations within a community of people who are connected by organic bonds; it is,
rather, a structure underpinning the contractual bonds of gold-
breeders and gain-seeking strangers, on which the trade and profit
of the city depend. Precisely because the law's purpose is primarily
commercial and not moral, it denies in this case, and in others, the
principle of mercy and it prevents even the Duke from intervening
with the spirit of 'human gentleness and love'. In the end, a
quibble allows Portia to reverse the injustice of the bond and
render Shylock helpless before *his* enemy, but it does not mitigate
the bond's amoral and hence immoral character. The fact remains that the law in this world-commercial context has been
transformed out of its role as an instrument of natural moral order
to become, instead, the instrument of my lord commodity, and
gain.

IV. CHAOS AND CREATION

Behind the transformation of the nature of bonds and kinds in
this historical epoch, lies the transformation of the concept of
nature itself. There is a steady progress, during the Reformation,
from the beneficent, reasonable, harmonious order envisioned by
the Middle Ages, to the Hobbesian view of Nature as malignant
and hostile, a perpetual war of appetites, *bellum omnium contra omnes*.

This fissure in the concept of Nature, which widened as the
century grew, paralleled the widening fissure in English society at

the time. 'For the two Natures . . . imply two societies. [One], . . . the new age of scientific inquiry and industrial development, . . . of mining and merchant-venturing, of monopoly and Empire-making, the age of the sixteenth century and after: an age of competition, suspicion, glory. . . .* [The other, a] society not yet outgrown. This is the society of the sixteenth century and before. . . . [Its standards] assume a co-operative, reasonable decency in man, and respect for the whole as being greater than the part: "God to be worshipped, parents to be honoured, others to be used by us as we ourselves would by them." ' †

The great confrontation of forces in *King Lear*, a play which probes 'nature' as its central question, involves in its essence the two conflicting conceptions of natural order. It is the Hobbesian nature of unrestrained appetite and self-will that Edmund invokes ('Thou Nature art my Goddess') and, in so doing, enters the main tradition of Shakespearean villains.‡ It is the counter-nature, aidant and remediate, to which Cordelia turns in her prayer:

CORDELIA: All bless'd secrets
    All you unpublish'd virtues of the earth,
    Spring with my tears. . . .   (IV. 4)

and to which Albany in desperation also appeals:

ALBANY: If that the Heavens do not their visible spirits
    Send quickly down to tame these vilde offences,
    It will come.

* 'The "three principal causes of quarrel" in human nature Hobbes found to be "competition, diffidence, glory": the impulse to acquire, to provide for one's security, to extend one's prestige'–John Danby, *Shakespeare's Doctrine of Nature: a Study of 'King Lear'*, London, Faber & Faber, 1949. On Hobbes's Nature as a model of nascent capitalist society, see C. B. Macpherson, *The Political Theory of Possessive Individualism: Hobbes to Locke*, Oxford, Clarendon Press, 1962.

† John Danby, op. cit. Professor Danby's book provided the basic inspiration for the present essay.

‡ E.g. Iago: 'Virtue! A fig! 'Tis in ourselves that we are thus or thus.' However, as Danby shows in his discussion of Edmund's ancestry, Shakespeare had a fine sense of the *virtù* if not the virtues of these figures and the new social order which they represented. If he was deeply critical, he was by no means undiscriminatingly so. Nor was he nostalgic for the old social order, whatever his regard for 'old' moral values.

Humanity must perforce prey on itself,
Like monsters of the deep.   (IV. 2)

The offences *are* tamed. Moments after Albany's appeal, a messenger enters with news that the Duke of Cornwall has been slain by his own servant while attempting to put out the Duke of Gloucester's eye:

A servant that he bred, thrill'd with remorse,*
Oppos'd against the act, bending his sword
To his great master, . . .

There is in anonymous humanity a principle that rebels when faced with inhuman deeds. This particular rebellion, moreover, like Pisanio's, is a rebellion against the social order in the name of a human order, which transcends society and gives it its authentic basis.

The vile offences are not only tamed by the 'Heavens' sending down', but by the very nature of the destructive potential itself. Goneril and Regan cannot contain their appetites and, in the end, prey on each other. Destructive evil cannot knit its forces into a viable and self-regenerating order. It is choked in its own chaos and eaten by its own appetite. It cuts itself off from its own springs of origin and as a result its issue is sterile and grows to naught:

ALBANY: That nature which contemns it origin
Cannot be border'd certain in itself;
She that herself will sliver and disbranch
From her material sap, perforce must wither
And come to deadly use.

Somewhere between this negative potential and its positive counterpart, the old king stands. Possessed, initially, by a tyrannic self-will, he does not embrace this attitude finally as a way, never irrevocably cuts himself off from the well-springs of human love and renewal. But in his odyssey of darkness he does explore something like the limits of the destructive will itself, before, by the grace of Cordelia, he issues from his tormented grave.

* Pity.

Lear is precipitated into his abyss because he fails to distinguish shadow from substance, flattery from love, false bonds from true, and hence because he embraces and empowers an order that is no order at all, that is a chaos.

> LEAR: Tell me my daughters,
> (Since now we will divest us both of rule,
> Interest of territory, cares of state),
> Which of you shall we say doth love us most?
> That we our largest bounty may extend
> Where nature doth merit challenge . . . speak . . .   (I. 1)

The idea that love is a thing, to be weighed up and measured for exchange, to be reckoned in market terms, that the best love can be bought at the highest price,* is basic to Lear's great error, and is a product of the false scale of his values. When Goneril and Regan later strip him of his hundred knights, his last vestige of power, he reiterates this false equation:

> LEAR: [to Goneril] I'll go with thee:
> Thy fifty yet doth double five-and-twenty.
> And thou art twice her love.   (II. 4)

But love cannot be calculated in this way (and indeed there is an element of bitter and pathetic irony in the word 'love' in Lear's speech). A relation, and not a substance, love manifests itself in answering the need of the other, not its own need to buy a good opinion for itself, a rich dowry. Because it is a relation, love cannot be measured, has no determinate extent, no currency value, no substance in the sense that gold has substance. It is not a thing; it is nothing:

> LEAR: [to Cordelia] Now our joy,
> . . . what can you say to draw
> A third more opulent than your sisters? Speak.

* He has, of course, divided up the lands beforehand. Nonetheless, the metaphor he chooses for his ceremony and, indeed, acts upon when Cordelia says nothing, reveals his basic outlook.

CORDELIA: Nothing, my lord.
LEAR: Nothing?
CORDELIA: Nothing.
LEAR: Nothing will come of nothing! Speak again.
CORDELIA: Unhappy that I am, I cannot heave
My heart into my mouth; I love your Majesty
According to my bond; no more nor less.   (I. 1)

Lear is unimpressed by Cordelia's bond. To him it is merely a negative binding: what she owes him. But she means the bond in its organic sense: she loves him as her father. What this means, Lear will learn at terrible cost; for it is precisely and poignantly this creative parental bond, a bond which by nature fosters a helpless nothingness into something, that, at the bottom of his abyss, he will so desperately need.

The quality of Cordelia's love is affirmed by the fact that it springs from a natural order. By contrast, that which Goneril and Regan initially show, pretending to 'love' Lear beyond and to the exclusion of all else, is without a root in nature: it is bound to the dower which he offers, and arises from the desire for it. Since the show of their 'love' is based on commodity, it vanishes when Lear has no more to offer them, and it is then that they really reduce him to nothing:

FOOL: ... Now thou art an O without a figure. I am better than thou art now; I am a Fool, thou art nothing.   (I. 4)

This is an essential truth for Lear, for his education and renewal. He has been told that he was everything. ''Tis a lie', as he has found out; he is not 'ague-proof'. 'Old age', he learns, 'is unnecessary'; he is nothing, and will return to nothing.

What redeems him from this nothingness? What comes to him in the hour of his great need, when, a 'ruined piece of nature', he has nothing any more to give? What gives him to himself?

GENTLEMAN: Thou hast one daughter,
Who redeems nature from the general curse
Which twain have brought her to.   (IV. 6)

A daughter's bond, unshakeable and tender, binds him to life:

> CORDELIA: How does my royal Lord? How fares your
>   Majesty?
> LEAR: You do me wrong to take me out o' th' grave;
>   Thou art a soul in bliss; but I am bound
>   Upon a wheel of fire, that mine own tears
>   Do scald like molten lead. . . .
> CORDELIA: O! look upon me, Sir,
>   And hold your hands in benediction o'er me. . . .   (IV. 7)

But it is Lear who stands in need of blessing, and, in a scene of unutterable pathos, it is *his* eighty-year-old unbending knees that kneel.

> LEAR: Do not laugh at me;
>   For, as I am a man, I think this lady
>   To be my child Cordelia.
> CORDELIA: And so I am, I am.
> LEAR: Be your tears wet? Yes, faith. . . .

He is amazed to see her weep for him, for he has done her such wrong ('Here I disclaim all my paternal care . . . property of blood, and as a stranger to my heart and me hold thee from this forever').

And then, in a touching recall of his early error, he utters disbelief of her love, which is really disbelief in the possibility of the 'payment' of a bond which he has not earned – indeed, which can never be 'earned' – a bond which is grace.

> LEAR: I know you do not love me; for your sisters
>   Have as I do remember, done me wrong:
>   You have some cause, they have not.
> CORDELIA: No cause, no cause.

Cordelia's love comes to Lear, in his most shattered hour, to answer his 'true need'. Love, as she gives it, is no exchangeable thing, but a power expanding as his need expands, growing as his need grows great.

In the depths of the tragic abyss, Lear envisions the dominance of the other of the two Natures. Nature is appetite –

> . . . die for adultery! No:
> The wren goes to 't, and the small gilded fly
> Does lecher in my sight. . . .   (IV. 6)

and power –

> A man may see how this world goes with no eyes. Look with thine ears: see how yond justice rails upon yond simple thief. Hark, in thine ear: change places and handy-dandy,* which is the justice, which is the thief?

The cause of this corruption and disorder in society is my lord commodity and his angel gold:

> LEAR: Through tatter'd clothes small vices do appear;
>   Robes and furr'd gowns hide all. Plate sin with gold,
>   And the strong lance of justice hurtless breaks;
>   Arm it in rags, a pigmy's straw does pierce it.
>   None does offend, none,

because all do offend.

> LEAR: . . . you see how this world goes.
> GLOUCESTER: I see it feelingly.
> LEAR: What! art mad?

To see feelingly, compassionately, is to risk madness in a world of such injustice, but it is also the only way to see that the play sanctions:

> GLOUCESTER: [to Poor Tom] Here, take this purse . . .
>   . . . that I am wretched
>   Makes thee happier: Heavens, deal so still!
>   Let the superfluous and lust-dieted man,
>   That slaves your ordinance,† that will not see

---

* The children's game of 'Handy-pandy sugar candy, which hand will you have?'

† Treats Heaven's ordinance with the contempt with which he treats his slaves.

> Because he does not feel, feel your power quickly;
> So distribution should undo excess
> And each man have enough. . . .   (IV. 1)

Gloucester's prayer for a redistribution of wealth parallels Lear's earlier prayer ('Take physic Pomp . . .').* The wisdom of the prayers is the same: it is what the thunder (justice) teaches them about the society of man, in the storm.

Thus Lear and Gloucester envision a possible redemption of man's social misery. But this redemption rests upon the restoration of human order, based on feeling sight, on the 'compunctious visitings of Nature', in essence, on a return to human kindness.

The forces that have seemed to support such a return are victorious politically at the end of *Lear*, but the destruction of Cordelia, who has been the active principle of redemption in this world, checks any hope that this victory raises. After *Lear*, when Shakespeare again touches on the social question, even the modicum of optimism present here is absent. My lord commodity reigns absolute.

But on another plane, a moral, or perhaps only symbolic plane, *Lear* does harbour a triumph. The reunion of Lear and his daughter means a healing of the breach between them and a 'rebirth' of the old man from his fiery and tormented grave:

> LEAR: You must bear with me.
>   Pray you now forget and forgive: I am old and foolish.
>   (IV. 7)

Thus, within the deepest, the most unbearable and dark abysm of Shakespearean despair, light breaks – there is warmth and human love; and this moment makes, in its own way, the rare miracle of the late romances, and confirms, in its own manner, their truth. For the myth behind these romances is the myth of Ceres and Proserpina, of a mother and child whose bond reaches down into the darkness of the underworld, whose separation is winter and whose reunion brings the return of spring. Children mean, in

* See above, p. 83.

their very beings, a beginning again, rebirth and renewal, and the bond of human love, which reaches beyond all boundaries and tenders forth something from a seeming nothing, this bond of human creation begets a human spring.

Index

acting, as metaphor, 39, 45, 82 f., 97
affection, 63n., 87
Alexander, 8
Antony and Cleopatra, 40 ff., 71, 82n.
appearances, 20 ff., 25, 30, 82
appetite, 7, 101 ff., 110 and n., 115, 123 ff., 129
Aristotle, 115n.
art, 46, 84, 95 ff.
As You Like It, 14 ff., 36 ff., 76 ff., 88, 91n., 96n.

Barish, J., ix
bond, 7, 32, 66, 95, 101 f., 108, 110, 114, 116, 119 ff., 127 f., 130
Buber, Martin, xii, 1, 4n., 7, 12, 44

celebration, feast, 16, 43, 59 f., 68, 78 f., 97
chastity, 95
Chiappe, A., ix, 14, 39, 42, 44n., 49, 71, 92, 93 and n., 95
commodity, 26, 112 ff., 122 f., 127, 129 f.
compassion, 78 f., 80 ff., 87 f., 92 ff., 125, 129 f.
Coriolanus, 71n.
Cymbeline, 91 and n., 102

Danby, John, 124n.
death, 35, 46 f., 51, 66 ff., 74, 96; and image of, 71 ff.
desire, and love, 6, 65, 103, 106 ff.
Diogenes, 8
Don Quixote, 17 f.
Dostoevsky, F., 7

endurance, 88 ff., 96

faith, 4, 12 f., 27 f., 108, 109 and n.
fertility, 42, 45 f., 67 f., 77 f., 82, 97, 130 f.

grace, xi, 9, 17 f., 68 ff., 77 ff., 81 f., 84, 86, 88 f., 95 ff., 127 f.

Hamlet, 1, 39, 81n., 88
harmony, 7, 15, 88, 93, 95 ff., 113, 123
Hobbes, Thomas, 123, 124n.
honour, 17, 63, 103, 104 ff., 106
hyperbole, romantic, 4, 6, 31 f., 34, 44, 64, 107

identity, 40, 56 ff., 62, 66, 69 f., 82 ff.

Johnson, Dr, 24
judgement, 71 ff., 86 f., 122
justice, 83, 88, 123, 129 f.

kind, 87, 117 f., 122
King John, 110 ff.
King Lear, 39, 72 f., 82 ff., 96, 124 ff.

love as direction, 18, 27 ff., 53 f.
love as relation, 4 ff., 26, 30 ff., 63, 126
Love's Labour's Lost, 77 f.

Macpherson, C. B., 124n.
market, 26 f., 121 ff., 126
Marx, K., 114n.
measure, 42 f., 67
Measure for Measure, 81n., 86n.
Merchant of Venice, The, 29, 87n., 115 ff.
Midsummer Night's Dream, A, 39

133